CONTENTS

PART ONE

Peace and Harmony

PART TWO

Egolessness

Contents

PART THREE

You Have to Say Something

Contents

Editor's Preface

Meeting Katagiri Roshi was like meeting a fresh morning breeze. He said things I had never heard before. He broke up the tired and worn tracks of my thought.

As I listened to him over the years, what he said was always new and fresh. Still, it was as though I already knew the things he was saying—a feeling many of us have when we are presented with what is Real. I knew he was pointing out Truth, though for several years I did not realize it.

When I finally saw what he was trying to show me, I was speechless. Whenever I tried to speak of it, I could not find the words. A year went by before I could say anything at all about it. At last I made a stumbling attempt to express the ineffable to him. I said, finally, "We can't talk about this." And he said, "You have to say something. If you don't speak, nobody will understand."

Katagiri Roshi measured up to his own demands. He was a prolific lecturer. For years he gave two Dharma talks per week—and a talk every day during meditation retreats. And each time he lectured, he expressed the inexpressible.

We have in this volume a collection of what he had to say about seeing Truth, and about how Zen insight is manifested in actual practice, in our actual lives, breath by breath.

We do not merely see, but we *live* Truth and Reality from moment to moment, whether we know it or not. With insight we can spare ourselves the pain of living with others but alone, and express the full realization that we live alone but as all beings.

Steve Hagen

ACKNOWLEDGMENTS

IT TAKES MANY PEOPLE to put a book together and many more when it is a book of this kind. From the hundreds of tapes of Katagiri Roshi's lectures and Dharma talks, a small army of transcribers converted the spoken word to print. I'd like to thank and acknowledge these people here.

We received the transcripts that were ultimately used in this book from Tom Bittinger, Clelia Corona, Matthew Eichenlaub, Dave Ellison (I should say *especially* from Dave Ellison, who supplied us with a great number of excellent transcripts), Larry Gross, Jan Hanke, Kay Hanson, Karin Jacobson, Joseph Janowski, King Kryger, Chanda Langford, Lynn Mennenga, Marianne Mitchell, Teijo Munnich, Lee Oatey-Crouse, Jennifer Patterson, James Patteson, John Pekins, Richard Reynolds, Ann Ruhlig, David Rumsey, Kurt Swanson, and Maureen Vivino.

Thanks also to King Dexter, Ted Meissner, Judy Melinat, Ann Milbradt, Neil Myers, Roger Pratt, Clarence Sharpe, and Kathy Sullivan, who did no less work in transcribing, but whose transcripts were ultimately not used here (though they may be used in future publications of Katagiri Roshi's teachings).

A few of the transcripts used in this text were made (in some cases many years ago) by people who never bothered to put their names to them. In some instances we managed to track them down, but in other cases we were unsuccessful. I want to thank them for their efforts.

Beyond the production of transcripts, there was the organizing of transcripts as well as transcribers. I would like to thank Jisho Cary Warner for pulling much of the material together in the initial stages of this book. A special thanks to Alice Erickson who, as coordinator of transcriptions, saw to it that we had plenty of material to draw from to form, shape, and edit into a book.

Thanks also to my Dharma brother, Norm Randolph, whose careful reading of the manuscript brought several improvements and corrections.

Last, but definitely not least, I want to thank Scott Edelstein, who was the catalyst behind this project and the glue that held it all together, as he worked with the Minnesota Zen Center board, Shambhala, Alice, and myself to bring this book to its completion. He acted as our agent and worked closely with me as my editorial advisor. He was indispensable in making this book ready for publication.

To all of you I am grateful. I believe that, together, we have produced a book worthy of Katagiri Roshi's teaching.

Steve Hagen

Everyday Life in Zen

How can we live according to Zen teachings? First of all, we have to do zazen—sitting meditation—on a daily basis. The important thing is not how long we sit—five minutes, ten minutes, fifty minutes, even one minute is okay. The important point is to let everyday life start with zazen and end with zazen. That is the first step.

Why do we have to do this? Because Zen *is* everyday life—to live day by day. And day by day is today—right now, right here. Right now, right here influences your whole life. To live life does not mean to live according to some spiritual or material idea. To live life—how you spend your life—means how you take care of life day by day.

According to the Zen way, you must be the master of yourself, whatever situation you may be in. You have to realize who and what you are. For this, all you have to do is concentrate on your hands, your feet, your eyes, your mind—in this present moment. In other words, when you do zazen, just sit down and concentrate on the breath—counting the breath or following the breath. When you have breakfast, just have breakfast. When you wash your face, just concentrate on washing your face. When you walk on the street, walk on the street. Zazen is a fundamental practice. It is about taking care of this moment with wholeheartedness. Just do it—right now, right here.

Daily routine is a huge, expansive continuation of routine activities—getting up in the morning, having breakfast, going to work, coming home, going to bed. Daily routine shows us how to live in this huge expanse of time, beyond any idea we may have of time. This is why everyday life—daily routine—is very important for us. It can let us be free from time.

But too easily we become fed up with daily routine. What are we doing, repeating the same things day after day? We don't like this. We fall into the trap of stereotyping human life as monotonous. We become interested in excitement and in breaking away from daily routine. This is very dangerous. We become confused and don't know what to do next.

We have to realize the true self that is free from this dangerous condition and we have to return to the true self.

To count the breath in zazen with wholeheartedness is to let time ripen. It is to be one with concentration, which is, strictly speaking, neither you nor concentration. At that time, you will neither bemoan daily routine nor be tossed away by unexpected occurrences. Thus we make every effort to do zazen on a daily basis. In return, zazen gives us a great opportunity to return to the true self.

If we are going to practice zazen in daily life, we have to think of it in a broad way. We need to do zazen with full concentration. When you do zazen, or anything else, do it with wholeheartedness. If you want to swim, jump into the ocean and swim with wholeheartedness. And when you jump in, both the idea of "swimmer" and the idea of "ocean" disappear. There is only the activity of swimming. This is no attachment. This is wisdom. Wholeheartedness means to do something with "no mind." It means to plunge into your activity and let time ripen, right now, right here.

To concentrate by means of one's ego-consciousness is to be confused. It is to be stuck in concentration. But when you concentrate wholeheartedly on your breath in zazen, full concentration naturally disappears in the rhythm of full concentration. This is to plunge into the ripeness of time—the activity of the moment. If you do this, immediately you are free from time.

If you do zazen with full concentration, immediately you are free from zazen, and from the idea of being someone who is *doing* zazen. Then there is nothing to debate: "Will I find something in zazen?" Or, "Will I forget everything from doing zazen?" Just give up any ideas. At that time, zazen becomes both empty and fully alive.

As I mentioned, it is easy to become fed up with daily routine. You do the same thing, day after day, until finally you don't know what the purpose of human life is. Human life just based on daily routine seems like a huge trap. We don't want to look at this, so we don't pay attention to daily routine. We get up in the morning and have breakfast, but we don't pay attention to breakfast. Quickly and carelessly, we drink our coffee and go to work.

But if you don't pay attention, you will eat breakfast recklessly, you will go to work recklessly, you will drive recklessly, and you will go to sleep recklessly. Finally, you will be fed up with your daily routine. This is human suffering, and it fills everyday life.

The important point is that we can neither escape everyday life nor ignore it. We have to live by means of realizing the original nature of the self right in the middle of daily routine, without destroying daily routine, and without attaching to it. When it is time to get up, just get up. Even though you don't like it, just get up. Getting up will free you from the fact that you have to get up.

Even though you don't like your life, just live. Even though death will come sooner or later, just live. The truth of life is just to live. This is no attachment. Zen practice is to be fully alive in each moment. Only by this living activity can you take care of your everyday life.

PART ONE

Peace and Harmony

Just take one step

EVERYONE LIKES ZAZEN AT FIRST. They feel that in zazen they can relax. But actually zazen is beyond tension or relaxation. If you do zazen, forget about relaxing and just sit down.

Regardless of whether you understand it or not, just do zazen with wholeheartedness, completely beyond any thoughts or speculations about obtaining any benefit. Just put all that aside and just sit. This is realizing Buddha. If you become a buddha, your body language speaks of your life—not merely of the little life you are living now in this moment, but of your whole life.

The important point is not to try to escape your life but to face it—exactly and completely, beyond discussing whether or not your zazen or your situation is good or bad, right or wrong. This is all you have to do.

One day, as the monk Baso sat in zazen, his teacher passed by and asked him what he was doing. "I want to become a buddha," said Baso.

His teacher immediately picked up a tile and started polishing it.

"What are you doing?" asked Baso.

"I'm polishing this tile to make a mirror," said his teacher.

"Ridiculous," said Baso. "How can your polishing make that tile a mirror?"

"How can your zazen make you a buddha?"

Baso's teacher really wanted to correct Baso's understanding of Buddhist practice. For Baso at that time, zazen was merely a means to an end. This is our common, dualistic attitude toward everything.

In the dualistic world, things always seem to exist in complete separation. They are never unified. But the dualistic world is created by human speculation. It is the world we conceptualize through our consciousness.

Human thought and speculation are not wrong, but they are often deceitful and evasive. When we are caught up in the dualistic world, we act just like a dog or a cat trying to get a piece of meat hanging from a pole tied to its own body. The moment it sees the meat, it goes for it, but of course it can never reach it. And the pole isn't stiff, but flexible, so that when the animal moves, the food snaps to the right and left, flying in all directions. This only makes the animal move all the more wildly.

This stuff dangling and moving in front of us is just noise created by our human consciousness. We enjoy getting lost in it, but it's deceitful, because it's dualistic.

To do zazen correctly is to transcend this dualistic world. Dogen Zenji said,

> The zazen I speak of is not learning meditation. It is the manifestation of ultimate Reality. Traps and snares can never reach it. You must realize that just there in zazen, Dharma is manifesting itself, and that from the first, dullness and distraction are struck aside.

Authentic practice of zazen is not a means to an end. It is an end in itself. This is why Dogen said it is not learning meditation. If you try to learn something through meditation, it becomes a means to an end. If you use zazen as a means, it is nothing but dust. Whether we think of it as iron dust or gold dust, it doesn't matter. Even if the dust that gets in your eyes is gold, it still hurts you.

Usually people have the idea that they can attain wisdom if they do zazen. But from the first, zazen is nothing *but* wisdom. If we don't understand this point, there is something stinky about our zazen. It is intellectual zazen—just the idea of zazen. It might look like zazen, but it is not zazen. It is just our everyday, helter-skelter mind.

According to traditional Buddhism, our helter-skelter state of mind must be subdued by the practices of *shamatha* and *vipassana*—tranquillity and insight. The first is to stop the helter-skelter mind and the second is to view the human world on a broad scale; in other words, to see it with wisdom. If we make our confused state of mind stop, we very naturally attain wisdom.

With wisdom we can see everything clearly. So at all cost, we have to make our minds quiet through these practices. But even though you may use these perfect practices of meditation, if you see them only as a means to an end, it's like kids playing hooky from school and wandering aimlessly through the streets. We don't want to look directly at life, at death, at zazen itself. We are always looking around for comedies and tragedies, but never do we look at life as it's being lived.

Zazen is not about destroying our thoughts or doing away with our subjective points of view. It's about how to deal with thoughts and views mindfully. In zazen, mindfulness, thoughts, and views all become simple and quiet because we are concentrated on just one thing, not many. At that time, mindfulness becomes very pure and clean, and our view becomes unified. When mindfulness, thoughts, and views all work together as one, this is zazen.

If you truly realize this, you can't be using zazen as a means to a happy future. You can only do zazen itself. Within zazen, all things work together and become one. There are no categories of good or bad, right or wrong, that can hold zazen. It touches the core of human life.

If you believe zazen is a means to an end, then it is easy for you to use zazen like a raft to reach the other shore. But if you get to the other shore like this, you won't know what to do next. If you use zazen in any way as a means to reach the other shore, you will never be satisfied.

At this point, people sometimes throw zazen away. "I've finished," they say. "I've reached the shore, so I don't need zazen anymore." But their life is still in a fog.

Sometimes people think they should carry their zazen around with them after reaching the other shore. But if you do that, you should know you haven't actually reached the other shore. You have just come up on a sandbar somewhere in the middle of the river. Desires are endless, and if you look carefully, you will see you are still caught by them.

If you carry zazen around as a means to an end, it will just keep getting heavier and heavier. If it's five pounds at the beginning, you might be able to carry it for a mile without trouble, but if you carry it for two miles, or three miles, or five miles, you will become exhausted. This is because your false shore starts washing away the moment you reach it. This is why you are not satisfied in zazen. You are still looking for the other shore.

This is just how most of us are confused. We don't appreciate the fact that desires are endless. We have to come to realize that there is nothing to get into our hands, and that zazen is not a vehicle, not a means.

So, how can we practice zazen as an end in itself? All you have to do is take a step. Just one step. Strictly speaking, there is just one thing we have to face, and nothing else. If you believe there is something else besides this one thing, this is not pure practice. Just take one step in *this moment* with wholeheartedness. Intellectually, we think about the past and the future, but if we take one step, this shore and the other shore are *now*. Taking one step already includes all other steps. It includes this shore and the other shore. This one step is zazen.

Just make your helter-skelter mind quiet and use mindfulness, thoughts, and views to see both life and death in this moment. Life is endless. But that's not important. What's important is that beginningless and endless life lies within a peaceful mind. Right now, right here, our life must be peaceful. To enter the gate of peace and harmony is not an idea. Like a falling leaf, it is the total manifestation of enlightenment and the illumination of ultimate reality.

settling in the vast openness of the sky

WE RECEIVE A LOT OF INFORMATION and thus have many things to deal with in our lives. This creates problems for us.

Look at how much information just comes from your head as soon as you sit down to do zazen. Your head is not small. It extends into the past, present, and future. So as soon as you sit down, your head starts to spin, and soon it's lost in thought. Information keeps coming so quickly that we can't stay with any one piece for very long. It just keeps coming up—one thing after another.

So, what good is zazen when your head always spins like that? Even just sitting, you're completely carried away. It leaves you thoroughly confused. This is why in zazen we must throw away all judgments and evaluations—all thoughts of good and bad, pros and cons. All we have to do is just sit down and completely open ourselves to right now, right here, without being carried away by all the information in our heads.

In Zen we often compare the thoughts in our heads to clouds in the vast openness of the sky. Clouds come and go, often in fascinating ways. Sometimes black clouds run wild in the sky, and heavy storms, even tornadoes, appear. Other times the clouds rise to lofty heights and shine in dazzling brightness. Occasionally our thoughts are so wonderful that they put all the buddhas and bodhisattvas to shame. At still other times, our thoughts are so horrible that we hide them in the shadows.

The sky embraces any kind of cloud and lets them all play freely. Unlike the way we try to deal with our thoughts, the sky is never carried away by the clouds. To live our lives fully from moment to moment, we must learn to settle into the vast openness of the sky. This is zazen.

To live fully is not to be puffed up with pride just because we see some cloud that looks like the Buddha's face. Nor should we be discouraged just because things don't turn out as we wish. In zazen we keep our posture straight, and we see both sides of every experience—enlightenment and delusion. Real zazen is when our bodies and minds are completely balanced.

So put yourself in the vast openness of the sky. Don't be tossed away by thoughts of enlightenment or delusion. Such thoughts are just information coming up from the past, present, and future. Our problem is not in the thoughts or the information: the problem is in us. We have to take care of this information and not be tossed away by it.

First, we must settle ourselves in the vast openness of the sky. Then we can see the fascinating clouds—both stormy and bright—in this vast and beautiful sky.

There's no escaping this moment

WHEN YOU SIT IN ZAZEN, how many beings sit with you? Right where you sit, many beings—emotions, thoughts, memories, physical sensations—appear from moment to moment.

Yet *this moment* is very simple. So why not just take care of it with all your heart?

But you can't. There are too many beings there, and they drag you away. If you see pain, pain drags you away. You try to make yourself relax because you are in too much pain. You start to think of other things you could be doing. Better things. Things that would bring you more benefit than just sitting here, doing nothing. But the idea of benefit is just another creature, sitting right here in that very moment. You think, "Oh yes, there *is* something better I can do. I want to do it!" But your body and mind are still just sitting here. It's only your thinking that has gone off wandering, stumbling over all the beings of the moment.

What about those persons who are facing death? Is their situation different from yours? There is really no difference. It is exactly the same. A man who was dying of cancer once told me his situation was like sitting zazen, because many beings would arise in each moment. I agree. No matter where we are, no matter what we face, we have to take care of *this moment*. That's all.

This moment is not the *idea* of this moment. If you see it as a concept, it becomes frozen. But the real moment is not frozen.

Whatever we may think about *this moment*, our practice is just to return to it. *This moment* is where all beings exist. Even though we have doubts and fears, even though we ask, "Why do I have to die?" no answer appears. Only *this moment* is Real. There's no escaping *this moment*. All beings—including doubt and fear—drop off in *this moment*.

Your situation is really no different from someone who is dying of cancer. When you see death, you will see that there is no escape from *this moment*. So what should you do? The only thing to do is to *see* and deal with *this moment* as it is—right now, right here.

Touching the source
of existence

THERE IS NOT MUCH COOPERATION in human society. We
hear people say things like, "That's not my job! You do it!"
This is not a good attitude. What we need is warm, horizontal
communication. Without this, life becomes pretty hard. We
will create stress for ourselves—and for no real reason.

We should encourage this kind of warm communication between people in our everyday life. We have to keep our eyes
open, not only to take care of our own tasks but to see how we
can help others. It is not enough, though, to understand this
in theory. If we don't really practice it, our life becomes fragmented and cold. Once we become cold, we require rules to
establish order. Then the rules become stronger and stronger.

In order to have warm human relations, we must pay attention to what is. In other words, we must touch the source of
existence. Only then can we take a deep breath; only then can
we feel relief.

Under all circumstances, we must be rooted in the source
of existence. Right in the middle of the dynamic unfolding of
our daily life, we must remain calm, quiet, and unperturbed.
Whatever praise or criticism you receive—either from yourself
or from others—there is no need to get bogged down in it. Just
be straightforward.

To accept life in a straightforward manner is to have a flexible mind, not clinging to ideas of good or bad, right or wrong.
We need to learn how solemn, dignified, and sublime human
life really is. No matter who we are, we should respect others
and not judge them. Nor should we judge ourselves. For example, usually we try to do something about our reputation. We
hang on to it when we should instead be learning how to free
ourselves from it. If you hang on to thoughts of your reputa-

tion, your mind will not be calm, because you are stirring up the water of reputation.

If someone slanders you, what should you do? Just make the waters calm. In other words, just forget it. This is not an easy practice. But if you hang on to the slander, you will become angry. You will fight. This just perpetuates the problem. This problem is not confined to slander or blame; it applies to praise and admiration as well. If you are admired, don't hang on to admiration. Just get on with what needs to be done.

If we are carried away by pros and cons, successes and failures, gains and losses, flattery and disgrace, we will not take care of our daily life. In order not to be carried away by these kinds of things, we must first touch the source of existence.

Stability, imperturbability, and tranquillity are not stagnant water. They are dynamic and active, and they are constantly working. They are life itself. We can't know them through ideas. Only through our actual experience can they be known. And only then do we touch the source of existence.

Holding fast and letting go

A FAMOUS ZEN STORY TELLS OF an old woman who took care of a monk for twenty years. Far from the village, in a hut she provided for him, the monk devoted those twenty years to practicing by himself.

One day the old woman decided to test the monk to see how well his practice had progressed. She asked her daughter to visit the monk's hut and tell the monk she loved him. The young woman pretended to pour out her heart to the monk, who responded, "A dead tree leaning against an ice rock / No warmth for the months of winter."

The daughter then returned to her mother and told her this story. The old woman became very angry. She went to the monk and told him his practice had not matured. Then she kicked him out and burned his hut.

I think many people misunderstand this story. The monk wasn't speaking literally of the cold months of winter; he was saying that he was not moved. He was saying, "Nothing ruffles me." In other words, while conditions were favorable, he digested all that came from the external world. But when conditions were unfavorable, he left without regret. There was no sadness in his departure, nor was there pleasure. All he had to do was leave in peace and harmony. There was nothing that hooked any of his senses.

We can easily merge with favorable circumstances, but what happens when we're faced with unfavorable circumstances? For example, if you are fired from your job and your whole world is turned upside down, what do you do? You must realize that right from the start, Reality is both favorable and unfavorable simultaneously. Our practice is to digest all the many things that come to us from the external world. Reality is vast. If you live according to Reality, then truly the circumstances under which you live cannot ruffle you.

It may be easy for us to do zazen under favorable conditions. That's fine. But we can't ignore unfavorable conditions. Whether we anticipate them or not, they keep coming up. It's not so easy to deal with our lives under unfavorable circumstances, but we have no choice. Both favorable and unfavorable are here now. The question is, what do we do when we're faced with unfavorable circumstances?

The totality of your life is beyond your capacity to judge and evaluate. There is always more than what you see in your evaluations. Even though you see yourself as lowly and far from Buddha, Buddha is not something separate from you.

To merge completely with what appears "out there" in the

external world is what we call Buddha. Understand that you are Buddha. But who is this Buddha? We don't know.

We must simultaneously hold fast and let go, right now, right here. This practice is difficult for us, but we cannot evaluate or judge it. For instance, we have to eat. This fact is beyond any thoughts or judgments we may have. The question is: How should we eat in Reality, right now, right here? Should we eat just to eat? Should we eat just to live? If so, why live? To make money? To become famous? To satisfy our personal desires? Whatever we say, it doesn't hit the mark. We can find no satisfying answer in words.

Everything is changing constantly. Furthermore, everything is interconnected, so whatever we pick up never shows itself to be just what it really is. Everything is alive. Both we and all the things in our experience are alive in each moment. Therefore, what we must do is just eat with all sentient beings. We have to eat with the deep aspiration to abide with all beings in peace and harmony, beyond judgment and evaluation. No one can force us to do this. It must come from our own hearts.

If I evaluate my zazen, very naturally the sense of good or bad comes up. I have already slipped from Reality. We have to go beyond judgment. After all our evaluating and judging and thinking, which keep us going in zigzags, we have to live. We can't ignore the objects that we see, but we can't stay with them either. We have to digest them; we must let them go.

The golden earth and the sweet, long river

IN CONCLUDING HIS ESSAY *Genjokoan, the Actualization of Ultimate Reality,* Dogen Zenji, the founder of the Soto Zen school in Japan, writes that "the wind of Buddhism makes manifest the great Earth's goldenness, and makes ripen the sweet milk of the long rivers." But when we look, it's difficult for us to see the world this way. Under our feet, the earth appears contaminated, and before our eyes the rivers are turbid. We have misgivings about the universe. We seem disabled by our cultural trappings and by our history.

It is not just mountains and rivers that are polluted—everything seems contaminated, disabled, ruined. And everyone is uneasy and afraid. But here, in the midst of such appearances, Dogen says the earth is golden and the rivers run with sweet milk. How can he say this?

It is only when we see things according to our individual perspective that life becomes filled with miserable events. With all our fighting and killing, we devalue human life. And once we devalue it, we find it easy to kill each other. This is our present situation. Yet we want to make a beautiful life for ourselves, and we hope for a peaceful world. But how can we have hope if we are creating misery?

Sometimes we say we will make every possible effort to live a good life, but beyond that we leave our lives up to fate. This may be a very common approach, but it is no way to conduct our lives. If you have this understanding, your life is like a boat drifting on a vast ocean.

Dogen likened life to riding in a boat. Most people just ride the boat of the universe. They are carried along, but they don't know where they're going. This is why people say, "We don't know what will happen in the future, so we'll leave it all to fate." This is to drift in the ocean. It's not so good. So Dogen is saying, "Please use a tiller, use a pole, take hold of an oar and row the boat." In order to sail across the ocean of human life and take our proper stance among the many beings of this world, we must see the earth as golden and taste the rivers as sweet milk.

If you don't understand, if you don't *see* any goldenness, you should open your heart and listen; you must accept the world in its entirety.

If you would practice the spiritual life, you cannot carry on just according to your limited understanding. To practice for the long run, you must have a profound aspiration to live your life in peace and harmony with all sentient beings. This is to take hold of the tiller, to grab an oar. It is called living in vow, aspiring to awaken each moment. To live in vow is to take care of the little details of life—like getting up in the morning. When it is time to get up, just get up. This is the way to enter the doors of a golden, peaceful world.

Getting up is only a tiny activity. It is not unusual—everyone does it. Although there is nothing outstanding about it, the goldenness of the earth is found in just such activities in everyday life. But instead of attending to such details, we form habitual ways of behavior by attending to our desires. This is no way to live. We will never satisfy ourselves through such means. If you really want to please yourself, just forget your longing and attend to your daily life. In this we find goldenness.

Peace and contentment are no big deal. They are right at our feet. But we have to carry them with us under all circumstances, beyond the satisfaction or frustration of our desires. In other words, the Buddhadharma is practiced just for the sake of Buddhadharma. Whatever happens, if you can do that, you will no longer drift in the ocean of human life. You will sail it.

This teaching is not limited to particular schools, sects, or denominations. It is universal. Whether you are Buddhist or Christian or something else, if you see the world with only a small, sectarian understanding, you will never find true peace. The truth is beyond any sectarian view. If you would live in peace and harmony with others, you must manifest your life in a universal way. This is your responsibility to the future. This is especially true for us today because we live in a world where many sects and denominations live very close to each other.

If we would have peace, we must find a universal way to manifest peace. We must together taste the sweet milk of the long river.

Ordinary people

As MENTIONED EARLIER, when Baso told his teacher that he sat in zazen because he wanted to become a buddha, his teacher immediately picked up a tile and began to polish it.

"How can your polishing make that tile a mirror?" asked Baso.

"How can your zazen make you a buddha?" asked his teacher.

In this dialogue, the tile stands for an ordinary person, while the mirror stands for a buddha. But if you believe a buddha is like a mirror, then you must always clean this mirror, because dust is falling on it constantly. In other words, you are judging a buddha to be an ordinary person, but even though you make every possible effort to become a buddha, you cannot do it—because an ordinary person is an ordinary person, and a buddha is a buddha. The essential quality of existence is completely beyond judgment and evaluation. No matter how long we try to become something else, it is impossible. We can't do it.

But just what is an ordinary person? Emptiness. And so, in Reality, we can actually be free from the identity "ordinary person." But we always handle "ordinary person" as though it were an object. We control and manipulate it as an object. In fact, we handle everything in this way—even spiritual things—and it all thus becomes the conceptual world of things and ideas.

The true nature of an ordinary person is completely beyond material or spiritual forms and explanations. All concepts must drop off if we would truly see the ordinary person. It is necessary that we see the ordinary person not as an ordinary person. We must ennoble, enhance, or raise each person and all things in the material world to their highest spiritual capacity.

We don't understand how sublime the ordinary person is. But eventually the ordinary person can become free from "ordinary person," because the true nature of the ordinary person is emptiness. It cannot be pinned down.

Compassion beyond opportunity

WHEN WE LOOK AT OUR LIVES, we generally pick out good aspects and bad ones. Then we criticize ourselves. Then we suffer. But even in the midst of our negative judgments, we still hold a positive view. For instance, imagine that I always take a negative view of my life. I always say to myself, "Hey, Katagiri, you are a bad boy." But as soon as someone else says, "You are a bad boy, Katagiri," I get angry, because I don't completely think I'm a bad boy. I still see some good boy here. So these two things are always coming up together.

Though criticisms constantly come up, we can't attach to either positive or negative views. We have to see the positives and the negatives as clearly as we can, accept them, and then continue with our lives—learning from our mistakes, forgiving others, and supporting others so that we may all live in peace and harmony. This is the literal meaning of *Dharma*—to support or to uphold all beings. When Dharma works in the human world, it is called compassion sometimes, and it is called wisdom sometimes. So wisdom and compassion are one.

Wisdom and compassion are very quick—so quick they create no gaps between you and your object. It is very difficult to see true compassion because it has no form. When compassion takes a form, it is just our idea of compassion. By working side by side with others, practicing kindness with our intention, wisdom works and compassion is given to others.

Sometimes, though, the compassion we offer doesn't work. This is when we limit our compassion by ideas or desires. This is okay. In order to learn real compassion, we have to experience both compassion that works and compassion that doesn't work.

Real compassion is like water coming up from the ground. It can be aroused in anybody. For example, if you see a baby fall into a well, your deep compassion is immediately aroused. Even before you think of how to act, you are acting to save the baby. But such a situation is rare. This is why we don't easily understand real compassion. We should pay attention to this kind of opportunity when it arises, because it has much to teach us.

We need to practice compassion every day. In observing our attitude toward others, we can learn to deal with all beings compassionately—with friendliness, attentiveness, and care. All we have to do is just continue expressing our compassion with our best intention, under all circumstances, day by day. Each moment gives us a great opportunity to extend compassion to everyday things and events. True compassion works beyond our intention. It is inconceivable and wondrous. It can manifest in even the most ordinary moment.

The diamond eye

THE NINTH CASE OF *The Blue Cliff Record* speaks of the "diamond eye,"

> which illumines and sees everywhere without obstruction. Not only can it clearly make out a tiny hair a thousand miles away, but also it can determine what is false and decide what is true, distinguish gain and loss, discern what is appropriate to the occasion, and recognize right and wrong.

The diamond eye sees through doors, through cushions, through trees—it sees all sentient beings.

To clearly make out a tiny hair a thousand miles away means that when you see a rock, you see the ocean a thousand miles away as well. If you truly *see* a rock, through the rock you can *hear* the sound of the ocean. In other words, to truly *see* is to *see* the whole world even through a small stone, without anything obstructing the view. To *see* the stone also means to take care of the stone exactly as it is—to take care of it along with all beings.

Though many beings exist thousands of miles away from you, you have to see them all. This doesn't mean merely to see them in your imagination. You have to manifest their reality right now, right here. If you can manifest the reality of all beings, then you can take care of this small stone as the manifestation of all beings. This is simply to awaken to all beings in this moment. In Buddhism this is called right choice.

On the other hand, if you don't take care of this stone but treat it as though it were separate from the rest of the universe, this is called wrong choice. This is our usual way, but it is delusion.

Whether you understand a stone as the manifestation of all beings or not, you have to *see* all sentient beings. Then you have to practice that *seeing,* moment by moment, day after day.

The Eightfold Path

THE NOBLE EIGHTFOLD PATH, as taught by the Buddha, consists of right view, right thinking, right speech, right action, right livelihood, right effort, right mindfulness, and right meditation. Each item uses the word *right*, but what is "right"? In Buddhism, Dharma is right. Dharma is the essential nature of being that makes it possible for all phenomena to exist.

In Sanskrit, the word for "right" is *samma*. It means "to go along with," "to go together," "to turn together." It originally comes from a term that means "to unite." So "right" is a state of being in which everything can live together, or turn together, united. Right is a state of human life in which we live in peace and harmony with all other beings. It is right, beyond our ideas of right or wrong, good or bad.

All sentient beings have the right to exist in this world in peace and harmony. Even harmful and disruptive people have the right to hear the Buddha's teachings, so that they might learn to live in harmony with the universal stream of life. Regardless of whether you are conscious of this stream or not, you are part of it, along with all beings. This is not a matter of discussion or criticism, because it is beyond our ideas.

The first aspect of the path is right view, or right understanding. The traditional understanding of right view is seeing and accepting the Four Noble Truths: the truth of the universality of suffering, the truth of the origin of suffering, the truth of the cessation of suffering, and the truth of the path leading to its cessation.

Our usual understanding comes from consciousness and activity. Consciousness forms concepts that divide and define the world in an effort to make things clear. Once we have things separated and defined, we analyze everything—philosophically, psychologically, and so forth. Finally, through the function of consciousness, we then try to unify everything once more. This unification of subject and object is called activity.

The question is, how can we unify the things that are analyzed by our consciousness, things that were never separate in the first place? With our usual understanding, we can't figure out what anything, including consciousness, is. Though we don't usually notice how confused we are, our usual view leaves us very confused about human life.

The Buddha always emphasized right view. Mahayana Buddhism gave special emphasis to the practice of giving, as well. This practice is the first of six fundamental principles of human life, which Buddhism calls the six perfections. In a way, the practice of giving is exactly the same as right view, because when you correctly understand human life, you will see that all beings are interconnected and interpenetrated with each other. With correct understanding, it is obvious that without such interconnection nothing can exist.

For instance, to say that Katagiri exists is to say that this Zen center exists and that Zen students exist. If you want to understand Katagiri, you have to understand Zen Center and Zen students and Minneapolis, and so on. Otherwise, you can't understand Katagiri. In the same way, if you want to understand yourself correctly, you should understand others, instead of always emphasizing yourself. This is the practice of egolessness. The practice of giving is the practice of egolessness. It is the giving of yourself.

The fundamental structure of consciousness consists of two aspects: one is self-assertion, the other is self-abandonment, or egolessness. It is to forget the self, as Dogen said. To forget the self, however, is to study the self, not to destroy the self. It is to help, enrich, and enhance others by completely going through yourself to touch the lives of others.

The primary characteristic of giving is self-abandonment, egolessness. If you throw yourself into your object completely and indisputably, without thinking of yourself, you will see everything as clearly as possible. This shouldn't be seen as self-sacrifice or self-disgust. It is something that helps and enriches others. To help others is to benefit the self. This is a characteristic of the perfection of giving, where neither giver nor receiver is seen. This is right view.

The second aspect of the Noble Eightfold Path is right thinking. For instance, suppose I decide I want to become a United States senator. First I should correctly understand myself, then I should think of where I am, then I should decide if it is possible. I am not now a citizen of the United States, so I would have to become one. Also, I should consider whether I have some capability as a politician. Do I have any? No, I don't. So I should let go of my desire to be a senator. This is right thinking.

Whatever you want to do, you are free. You can do anything. But Zen teaches us to be compassionate and kind to all sentient beings. Maybe you want to help people who are starving. If this is what you want to do, why don't you do it now? Of course, it's impossible to help all the people who are starving. So you should first understand where you are and what is possible. This is right thinking. If you understand where you are, then you can help, little by little.

The next aspect is right speech. This is to be prudent, polite, kind, and compassionate in what you write and say. And right action is to be compassionate and watchful in what you do. Keep a careful watch over your behavior. Right action involves not only your body but your mind as well.

Right livelihood is about living in peace and harmony with all sentient beings. Practicing right livelihood is the best way to educate people about Buddhism. If you want to be a Buddhist, when you visit your parents, don't argue with them. If they are Christian and you put down Christianity while talking about how great Buddhism is, you don't understand Buddhism. Instead, keep your mouth shut. Why don't you just be present with your parents in peace and harmony? Sooner or later, they will be interested in what you are doing.

Right livelihood also involves choosing your occupation. Sometimes you have no choice but to have an unhealthy or harmful occupation. But whatever one's occupation, it is not a matter for criticism. If you criticize those with harmful occupations, you become disharmonious. Whatever the occupation, just be present in peace and harmony with all sentient beings. Don't criticize others.

Right effort means that if you start to do something, do it completely. Right effort is not to press on too much and not to withdraw. It is just to be present. If you press on recklessly, you will become exhausted. If you withdraw, you will leave things half done. Just be present.

Right mindfulness is to find yourself in what you are doing. In painting, in playing music, in doing zazen, be mindful of what you are doing. Find yourself in your activity. When you paint, painting is your life. When you do zazen, zazen is your life.

Finally, there is right concentration. This is to climb to the highest point and look at the overall situation of this moment, where you can observe your whole life and truly see what you are doing. When you do this, your mind becomes calm. If you are not calm, you will act like you are trying to escape a dangerous situation. You will move indiscriminately, like a panicky person who is lost in a forest. When you find that there is truly no security in life, you will become very confused and will likely run wild in all directions to escape the forest.

But this is not the way to escape the forest. If, instead, you climb the highest tree and look at the overall picture of the situation you are in, then you can see where to go. All you have to do is just climb the tree and see the total picture of human life. This will calm your mind and enable you to live with all sentient beings in peace and harmony.

Refined action

WE SPEAK OFTEN OF "PRACTICE" or "training." But these are very different from the term used by Dogen Zenji. Buddhist practice is not mere training as we commonly think of it.

Generally speaking, we think of human actions in moral terms, and we label them "good," "bad," or "neutral." But in Buddhism, we think of actions as needing refinement. This is to view our actions in a way that is completely beyond our ideas of good or bad. From this standpoint, practice is very different from what we commonly mean by the term.

We tend to see practice in terms of time—as if we were climbing a ladder step-by-step. This is not the Buddhist idea of practice. When you climb a ladder, you do so with your eye on the future. With this approach to practice, there is no peace, no spiritual security—only a hope for the future. We always feel we have to press on. But the more we try to find peace and happiness in this way, the further off they seem. There is often a lot of excitement but no peace. This is our usual human life.

Refined action is not like this. From the start, it lies in peace and harmony. To express this, Dogen used a peculiar term: *gyoji*. *Gyo* means "action"; *ji* means "to maintain," "to keep," "to sustain," or "to preserve." The character *ji* has two parts: one is "hand," the other is "sanctuary." *Sanctuary* here means the universe. Wherever you may be, your life is sustained and supported by the whole universe. The main purpose of human life is to maintain this sanctuary. It is not to climb a ladder to develop your own personal life.

If you see refined action or nirvana or enlightenment, or even the aspiration for enlightenment, in terms of time or progress, your understanding is not correct. These four are without beginning or end. They are like a circle, where the beginning is the end and the end is the beginning. As Dogen said, there is not the slightest break between them. This is where peace and harmony prevail; this is Buddhist practice.

Dogen also points out that refined action comes neither from your effort nor from someone else's. If your effort were not supported by the universe as a whole, you could not make any real effort at all. Pure, refined action makes no distinction between self and others. Trees, birds, and all other beings are completely harmonized in this sanctuary of the whole. This is our life.

Nothing to depend on

I THINK MOST PEOPLE HAVE DOUBTS about the practice of zazen. Compared with other practices you can learn in various workshops and seminars, just sitting seems too simple to touch our hearts. Thus it seems too difficult as well.

For this reason, most people ignore this simple practice of just sitting and take up other things more fascinating. We go for the mysterious experiences of the spiritual life in order to satisfy our individual desires. But whatever we experience when we seek to fulfill our spiritual desires—whether through workshops and seminars or even through zazen—it never hits the mark. It is always shaky.

For example, even though you feel good in your zazen one moment, in the very next moment it is gone. Feeling good is very unstable. We always forget about change. This is why most people are so restless. And this is why so many of us try to find something to help us settle down. Unfortunately, the more we try to settle ourselves, the more we feel unstable, and then we look for still other practices to help us. The practices we run to are endless. But no matter how long we spend in this cycle of frustration, we must finally come to the realization that we live right now, right here. That is, we have to live in a way that is beyond all human speculation. We have to learn to live with an imperturbable mind.

Isn't there anything we can depend on? Something we can do to benefit ourselves psychologically, or spiritually, or philosophically? Can't we find relief through some teaching or some person? No. There is nothing.

But there is one thing we can do. We can learn to live right now, right here, right in the midst of the circle of life and death, which Buddhists call samsara. All we have to do is make our life stable, be present in the endless repetition of life and death, and just live from moment to moment. This is all we can do. There is nothing else. This is life. This is death. Life and death are not two.

_____ The secret in your heart

BUDDHISM TEACHES US that life and death are One; Truth and transitory phenomena are One. Accept your life from beginning to end. This means to accept your death as well. Receive both life and death straightforwardly, without any doubt or hesitation.

Many religions use other terms to explain the Oneness of Truth and phenomena and of life and death. But whatever terms we use—Oneness, Truth, God, Buddha—they are far from us. They don't touch our hearts. This is why Dogen Zenji often used the term *intimacy*. He didn't mean physical intimacy, or even mental intimacy. He meant something beyond these. Sometimes he used the term *intertwined*, in the sense that a vine is intertwined with other vines. Dogen used this term to show how, beyond our *ideas* about life and death, our life and death is already intimate with Truth as a whole.

If you go to a Zen monastery in Japan, you will see a little wooden gong with this verse written on it: "Life and death are impermanent and swift." Whether they understand it or not, all monks see this verse. And though it can be explained very simply, the verse is considered a secret.

It is a secret because most people don't understand it. And without understanding, this teaching is not intimate, or intertwined, with most people's lives. But this teaching is very important for us, so it should be open to everybody. Fully realizing that both life and death are impermanent and swift is essential to seeing the Truth of human life.

Life and death is a great matter, and we must all deal with it. Not only are people, animals, and plants subject to life and death, so too are mountains, pebbles, and springtime. Life and death is not something mystical or secret. If you accept life and death without any conditions, your life will become supple instead of rigid. You will not create strife.

But most people are exploited by life and death. They first make themselves rigid, and then they try to get out of being rigid. This doesn't work very well, because the more you try to stop being rigid, the more rigid you become. During zazen, if I tell you, "Don't think, just sit," you start to think, "I shouldn't think." But the more you try not to think, the more you think.

Most people handle their lives in a backward way. They don't realize the origin of life and death. They always involve themselves with things and issues far from where their life actually blooms. But if you accept life and death straightforwardly, you will be flexible, generous, and forgiving of others in any circumstance.

My teacher didn't teach me anything. He only devoted himself to his everyday routine. He was just like a river—always flowing. He was aware of everything I did, but he didn't say anything. Finally I couldn't stand it, so I complained. I told him I wanted to give up being a monk.

I had two reasons. First of all, it was very boring. I was eighteen years old and had lots of energy, at least lots of physical energy. Psychologically, however, I was completely exhausted.

The second reason was that I was curious about the Pure Land school of Buddhism. My family was of that school, so I knew their ways. And I hated Zen.

When I told my teacher that he didn't teach me anything, all he said was, "Why didn't you ask me?" And when I told him I wanted to give up being a monk, he didn't scold me. All he said was, "Wherever you may go, everything is the same."

Sometimes students ask me if they should go to San Francisco or Japan or other places, or if they should stay here. But no matter how long we discuss the question "What should I do?" there is no conclusion. You must just be here. "Here" doesn't mean Minneapolis or San Francisco. "Here" means right now.

There is nowhere to go. This is liberation. It's very simple. Too simple. If you touch it, it's gone. Freedom is very intimate. It's like a secret in your heart.

Facing life and death

IN BUDDHISM, LIFE AND DEATH are not separate; they walk as one. Life is death; death is life. This is very difficult to understand. That's why we have to meditate on the problem of life and death every day, year after year.

There was once a man who sent for the Buddha because he was dying of some illness. When the Buddha came, the man tried to get up from his bed, but the Buddha asked him to stay put. Lying there, the man said to the Buddha, "My situation is said to be hopeless. I just wanted to see your face once again before I die and pay my respects to you."

The Buddha said, "It is of no use to see my body, which is going to rot and fade away. Instead, consider this: if you see Dharma, you see me; if you see me, you see Dharma."

The Dharma—Truth, Reality—never changes. It is the unified ground upon which life and death, good and bad, movement and stillness, all coexist, interwoven, peacefully and harmoniously, with no separation between them. This means that when we see life, death can be found in it. And when we see death, there is life.

Since they are so thoroughly interconnected, it is impossible to see them both at once. Nevertheless, we can learn to see this one ground, where all opposites coexist and work together without confusion. In other words, life is still life, and death is still death. Together they totally manifest the Dharma, without excess or deficiency. Thus, when death comes, it is perfect, for it contains life. It is not necessary to compare it with life. And when life comes, it is not necessary to compare it with death. Life holds death. Yet life is life, with no deficiency. All we have to do is take care of life and take care of death, day by day, from moment to moment.

There's a story of Zen master Ungan, who was hard at work sweeping the temple yard. Zen master Dogo came to him and said, "You're working hard."

"There's a name for people who don't work hard," said Ungan.

"If so," said Dogo, "there are two moons."

"Two moons" refers to our dualistic understanding of the world and of ourselves. With such thinking, there seem to be two kinds of people—hardworking and not hardworking. But sweeping the temple yard doesn't take place according to our dualistic views of hardworking and not hardworking. All is still. There is no movement to be found in Reality. So Ungan sweeps in movement that isn't movement. In other words, he sweeps in the unified ground where hardworking and not hardworking take place at once, without excess or deficiency. This is Dharma.

If you sweep the temple yard while standing on this unified ground, you can see clearly how the world goes on from moment to moment. This is wisdom; this is spiritual security. To sweep thus is the manifestation of wisdom. It manifests on the surface of the world. But when your life is backed by wisdom, you can see the depths of the world's activity. Then, in every moment you sweep, you sweep with wholeheartedness.

If you see your action in a dualistic sense, even slightly—working hard or not working hard—confusion arises in your mind. Your mind is always going here or there, to the right or to the left—always attempting to leave here and now, to look for purpose or meaning beyond itself. Like so are our endless discussions of life and death. There is no resolution.

There was once a teacher who went to see a student who was dying of cancer. She said her heart was screaming, and she couldn't stand it. The teacher said, "Let go of it." He repeatedly told her to just let go. But she said, "I can't let go of it!" And so, immediately, the teacher said, "Then let it come in." He understood: it is the same thing. Shortly thereafter, the student died peacefully.

Dealing with life and death is not a matter of discussing how to help those who are about to die. This teacher knew that, and therefore his words were not merely words—they were the total manifestation of a life based on many years of practicing the Dharma.

In Dharma there is nothing to hold on to because, in Reality, life and death work together. We can't hold on to life; we can't hold on to death. If you see them as separate, you create a crack between them. You give them a defining edge, and you try to take hold of them. Then you compare this with that. But whatever you think, however much you scream, the disease, the cancer, life and death—all go on beyond the world of attachments that you create. You must learn to deal with death without attaching to it, without holding on to anything at all.

This is not so easy. That's why the woman said she couldn't let go. She lived with a scream that came from the bottom of her heart. But no matter what we say or do, the Dharma world—the true world—just goes on. Through birth and death, it goes on. So if you can't let it go, then let it come in. To let it go, to let it come in—both are the same. You can't attach to either one, but you have to do something.

To say "Let it go, let it come in" is exactly the same as the Buddha's statement "If you see Dharma, you see me; if you see me, you see Dharma." Such words come from learning the nature of emptiness and from seeing what life and death truly are. These words don't come from entertaining ideas about how to help the person who is going to die. No ideas are of any use here. All you can do is show yourself totally and demonstrate the whole of your life right in front of the person who is about to die.

Today we are more interested in counseling people on how to become more peaceful as they face death. This is good, of course, but it is not the most urgent thing. What is more urgent is that *you* must be one who has truly digested life and death. Otherwise, how can you help others who are facing life and death?

Because we all face life and death—and not just once, but every day—it is vital that we meditate on the problem they present. Don't be frightened. Just face it directly. This is our practice. There is no other choice.

Inconceivable cosmic life

A STUDENT SENT ME A LETTER that told the story of a Chinese nettle tree in Hiroshima, in an area called Motomachi. The tree was struck by the blast of the atomic bomb that was dropped on Hiroshima in 1945. It had no branches or leaves, but at the beginning of May 1985 it began to put out buds. A sign in front of the tree reads:

The atom bomb turned even this Chinese nettle tree into an ugly thing. It has continued to survive until today. The poor little tree has known the strength and value of life. We who live in Motomachi have a duty to protect this tree.

—*The Motomachi Primary School Children Association*

Over the years, the children of this school carefully protected this tree. In 1982 an old tree surgeon named Yamano heard about the tree. He was known for having previously revived nearly nine hundred old and famous trees, and it was said that he could tell if a tree was still alive just by feeling it. According to Yamano, trees know the hearts of people. He also says that trees will keep on living, if they are allowed.

The nettle's only remaining root was the main one at its center. All the surrounding roots had withered away. But as soon as Yamano touched the tree, he knew he could revive it. He dug deep around the central root, injected a nutritional solution, and filled in new earth. He told everyone that the tree would put out new buds without fail. Then he left.

As he promised, the tree put out buds.

The life of this tree is inconceivable. But it is not just this tree whose life is inconceivable—humans, rocks, birds, air, and all beings have the same universal, cosmic life.

When we see a tree with just our physical eyes, we make judgments about it and speculate on the nature of its life or its death. Like so, we make judgments about everything—rocks, birds, other people, and so on—based on our notions of what is alive and what is dead. But we ignore the great, vast, and inconceivable life that is, behind our ideas of life and death. From this perspective, the life and death we commonly distinguish are not different. Even though we may call something dead, this is not Real death. There is actually life there. The Chinese nettle gives us a good example. For forty years it was a dead tree, and then it bloomed.

Instead of being tossed about by our speculations about life and death, we have to take responsibility for our capacity to see inconceivable life. In Buddhism we have the practice of *shamatha-vipassana* meditation. *Shamatha* means "tranquillity" or "stillness"; *vipassana* generally means "insight." But *vipassana* actually has two meanings. One refers to what we can experience through our bodies and minds—what we call worldly experience, or worldly truth. The other means direct participation in inconceivable life.

It may seem helpful to use *vipassana* merely as a means to participate in inconceivable life. But that is not the final goal. The final goal is that your worldly life must merge with inconceivable life through actual realization. Before we conceptualize and separate ourselves from the world, there is something inconceivable. There is already universal, cosmic life. It is why you are alive.

Just remember the Chinese nettle tree. According to our judgments, the tree was dead. Yet it was actually alive. But where is this life and this death? They worked together for forty years. They work together still, as they do in all things.

There is a power in the Chinese nettle tree that is not a part of the tree. It is not inside the tree nor is it outside. Whatever we may think about this, beyond our ideas of the life or death of this tree, there is an inconceivable world supporting this tree and allowing it to survive. It is a place where life and death work together, beyond all our thoughts and speculations. Although we don't know how, after forty years the dead tree blooms.

We listen to such stories and judge them impossible. But despite all our judgments, the dead tree blooms. This is why we sit in zazen. In the truth of zazen, life and death are merging, moment after moment. And thus, because our lives are supported by all beings through the merging of life and death, we bring forth inconceivable life.

Tamed and untamed
consciousness

THROUGH OUR SIX SENSES (including the mind) we experience form, sound, taste, smell, feeling, and thought. We might think we understand these things, but perhaps our common understanding is insufficient. For example, take feeling.

The Buddha spoke of subtle feeling, which is the Oneness of our feeling and the object of our feeling, *before* they are dichotomized. This is the very first stage of feeling. Subtle feeling is beyond the reach of our judgments, our criticisms, or our evaluations. Our usual feelings can be classified into several categories: physically or mentally pleasant, unpleasant, or neutral. But subtle feeling occurs *before* such judgments are made. It is the state of Oneness with our object.

We might think it is impossible to have such feeling. But we only think this because we have been tamed, or educated, by the dualistic world. The fact is, subject and object—you and what you touch or feel—are One from the start. Realization is only a matter of *seeing* that this is so. Until we *see* in this way, we assume we are existing together with many beings in a world of good and bad, right and wrong. But actually, if we would just look carefully at our experience, we would *see* that all beings *already* exist together in peace and harmony, without disturbing each other in the least.

From the perspective of everyday human consciousness, the world seems to consist of many competing things. This consciousness divides and separates everything. It makes distinctions. This way of seeing is why we never really understand anything as it is. We're not One with the flow of *this moment*. This moment, as it is, is already Oneness.

At its first stage, feeling is just Oneness. It's One with the flow of instants as they are. Then we say there is instant A and instant B. But the "A" and "B" we pick out are just the dregs—

the remains or results—of what we have experienced. They are already past. Gone. Not real. They are not *this* instant itself, because *this* instant is always in motion.

But though we can't attach to A or B as an instant of time, we can't ignore them either. We should accept them, but we need not be caught by them. All we have to do is participate in the flow of *this instant*—that is, we have to just be here.

Of course, we *are* here already. But we always pick up something in particular. This is our consciousness at work—it's very quick to pick something up. It then forms a pattern by which, over many years, we become tamed—educated into believing that what we pick up is Real. Then we completely forget this process of the instants of time, of action that lives from moment to moment. We have to realize this process of instants, learn to be present in *this moment*, and put this learning into practice. This is a big project for us, but it is of utmost importance.

Life we're living now

WE SEE OUR PERSONALITY as a single thing, but it is multifaceted, combining in various ways emotions, will, feelings, volition, and intellect. As it unfolds in our everyday life, it includes a multitude of ideas of who we are and who others are. We evaluate ourselves and we criticize others; we criticize and evaluate our own situation as well. Thus we create anger, hatred, and conflict in our lives.

But beyond our evaluating and criticizing, something else about us still speaks. What is it? We can call it whole personality. The whole of our personality extends far beyond the limits of our conventional personality, and we can be characterized as the space that surrounds us—to our front, our back, our right and left, above our heads, and beneath our feet.

With our intellect we judge others and analyze the world. But our intellectual understanding is just a speck of dust compared with our whole personality. The problem is that our intellect believes that its own understanding is perfect. Our intellect is like the space directly in front of us where everything is clear, understandable, and reasonable. We like this space and give it most of our attention because we always want everything to be clear and neat. We don't want to deal with those aspects of the world that are dark and murky.

We don't like what we don't understand, so we try to understand everything. What we can't understand, we ignore, and fool ourselves into thinking we understand more than we do. We ignore what we don't see, just as we ignore the space that is to our back. But it's a huge space.

If we liken the space in front to the bright world of the intellect, then the space behind us is very dark. Although we don't understand what's going on there, we continuously carry it with us. It is our past, our future, our heredity, our questions about life and death. We can't get rid of it.

The space of our personality also includes the spaces to our right and left. These are the spaces of our human relationships. The space under our feet is our everyday life. Finally, there is the space above us, which is beyond what we normally see. It feels good to look up when we are really confused. This is why people look up when they pray. This space is vast, clear, open, and wonderful.

If you want to live in peace and harmony, you have to accept all these different kinds of spaces. But our intellectual understanding tells us that we stand apart from everything, from the space around us. So we must change the intellectual patterns that we've become used to. This means parting from our head, and feeling those aspects of human nature that we don't know intellectually. We shouldn't try to throw the intellect away, but we must take care of it properly.

For instance, our intellect believes that there is nothing

after death, that when our skin, muscle, and bones decay, our consciousness will be no more. We believe that death takes everything away, that nothing will be left, not even the world. But is this true? If we truly believe that nothing remains after death, we will not be satisfied. Our intellects push us to understand what the world is. As we research this, we begin to compare this world with other worlds. But in the end we only end up chasing after what we have put there ourselves. We become like a dog chasing its own tail.

This is the nature of the world of the intellect. But there is more to the world than our intellectual understanding. If we understand our whole personality, then we can find the world of the heart. For this we have to make our minds calm. With a calm and balanced mind, we will be able to touch our whole personality and go beyond a mere intellectual understanding.

Dogen says that mountains are not mountains, birds are not birds, trees are not trees. Although we don't believe it, each thing and each system is cosmic in its reach. We always believe that a tree is just a tree. We say, "I know it," but we don't *Know*.

Even if we try to solve the problem of life and death by saying there is another world beyond death, it's still not good enough, because no one has ever proved that such a world exists. Though we dig through books on religion and philosophy, though we study the words of sages, though we believe it completely, there is still no proof.

In Buddhism we have stories of places where we might go after death—cold hells and hot hells, realms for hungry ghosts, fighting spirits, heavenly beings, animals, humans, bodhisatt-vas, and buddhas. But how do you know what kind of world you will experience after death? Instead, why don't you just live your life as it is right now, in each moment? No matter how long you research other worlds, you still don't know if you can depend on them.

Though Buddhism mentions other worlds, they are not necessarily worlds that appear after death. These are worlds that exist now. If you are a bodhisattva now, then you belong to the bodhisattva world, practicing the Buddha's teaching very peacefully. In the next moment, you might leave the meditation hall, go out on the street, and get into a fight. Immediately, you have entered one of the hell worlds.

We always live now. All we have to do is entrust ourselves to the life we now live.

Bodhi Mind

BODHI MIND TRANSLATES LITERALLY as "enlightenment mind," but it is known by many names. The great teacher Nagarjuna, for instance, called it "the mind that sees into the transient nature of the world." Though Bodhi Mind is known by many names, they all refer to One Mind. Bodhi Mind is not one's individual mind. It is universal Mind, and it is open to all beings. It is Mind with a capital *M*. It is the state of enlightenment.

In the *Prajna Paramita Sutra*, Bodhi Mind is short for "unsurpassed, complete, perfect enlightenment." This refers to a state that includes all sentient beings. According to the Buddha's teachings, all beings are enlightened, all are Buddha. So, to arouse the Bodhi Mind is to awaken to this Truth. Dogen Zenji said we must be continually mindful of this if we are to arouse Bodhi Mind. Under all circumstances—walking, sitting, standing, reclining—wherever we may go or whatever kind of situation occurs in our lives, whether favorable or unfavorable, we must continually be mindful of the truth that we—and all beings—are Buddha.

This is pretty difficult for us. We can live the truth that we are Buddha under favorable conditions, but it is not easy when conditions are unfavorable. Still, as Dogen Zenji said, we have to do it, constantly.

In *The Record of Things Heard,* Dogen says:

> When your aspiration to seek the Way has become sincere, either during a period of sole concentration on sitting, or when dealing with illustrative examples of the people of olden times, or when meeting the teacher, when you act with true aspiration, though your aim be high you can hit it, though it be deep you can fish it out. With this mind so forcefully earnest, there can be no failure of attainment.

Bodhi Mind is a strong, steadfast aspiration to seek Truth. This is the purpose of practice, the purpose of the spiritual life. "To arouse this determination," said Dogen, "it is necessary to earnestly contemplate the impermanence of the world." We have to see the truth of how transient the world is and how fragile human life is. Impermanence is the Truth that everything, without exception, *is* motion. There is just continuous change. Your body and mind—all things—are nothing but change itself.

Dogen goes on to say that "this task is not something that is to be considered as a temporarily prescribed method of contemplation. And it is not that you should invent something nonexistent to think about. It is Truth in Reality right before your eyes." In other words, impermanence is not an idea. It's Real. It is right in front of you, now. Your body and mind are nothing but impermanence. But we generally see impermanence as an object. We don't see it as ourselves. Though we understand it intellectually, we don't touch it directly. We don't really see how impermanent we truly are.

You are a buddha, so learn to behave as a buddha. Go beyond your self-centered ideas, your likes and dislikes. At that time, your natural capacity will mature, and you will manifest your true nature in your everyday life.

Buddha's mind

THE BUDDHIST PRECEPTS are not commandments. They are not moralistic rules that deluded people are expected to obey. Actually, the Buddhist precepts are not rules at all.

They should not be seen from a deluded point of view. Rather than see them as moral dictates to be followed, we should regard them as indicators of the practice of enlightenment. They should be taken as the Buddha's mind. If you do this, you can behave as a buddha.

This same attitude applies whenever you study under someone who has mastered an art or discipline. For example, if you want to master calligraphy, you should study the work of a great calligrapher. Of course, if you compare your calligraphy to the master's, it looks inferior. But if you say you would rather write in your own style, you will never progress. You don't know how long it will take you to master the art of calligraphy, but if you continue to study the works of the great calligraphers, you will reach a point where the true strength of your practice will be actualized. Before you are conscious of it, you will master calligraphy. And then your hand will move naturally.

At the beginning of practice, you might believe the precepts are moral rules. But you must learn to take them as expressions of the Buddha's activity. In doing so, you will study your everyday life, and before you are conscious of it, these teachings will penetrate your life. In this way, you can live naturally the life of a buddha.

The first two precepts are to refrain from what is unwholesome and to practice what is wholesome. The third precept is to purify your own mind. In order to perfect these, and the other precepts, we have to sever three ties. The first of these is doubt, or wrong view, which occurs whenever we attach to our cherished or tightly held ideas.

In Buddhism, human life is seen in light of the teachings of impermanence and cause and effect. These teachings seem contradictory, but actually they work together. On the one hand, everything is impermanent, so there is nothing we can grasp or cling to. On the other hand, there is cause and effect. If you do something, it will very naturally have results. These two seeming contradictory teachings account for much of why we are confused by human life.

Whatever we plan for our lives, we must take impermanence into account. It's a basic fact of existence. Impermanence doesn't have any form or color or smell. We only see it in the process of continual change. It's a kind of energy—always moving, functioning, working. This impermanence—this continuous movement, change, this appearance and disappearance—is what supports our lives. We have to care for our lives with impermanence in mind. We cannot attach to the results of what we plan.

People tend to ignore these teachings of impermanence and causation. This is called wrong view. But we have to accept them. They are facts of life.

The second tie to be severed is selfishness. To be selfish means we attach to our self as our first concern. It's very difficult to be free of this.

The story of the tortoise and the hare illustrates how to be free of this kind of attachment. The tortoise is one of the slowest creatures in the world, yet in the story the tortoise beats the hare in a race. Common sense tells us that he could never win a race with a hare, but he did. But consider the enormous effort the tortoise had to make. He had to free himself completely from the label of being the slowest creature. He had to make every possible effort just to move. Instead of expecting some particular result from his effort, he had to just walk forward, step after step.

In order to make such effort ourselves, there are three things we need to do. First we have to free ourselves of any kind of judgment or label, such as "I am poor," "I don't have any capability," or even "I am very capable." Forgetting all these, all we need to do is just make an effort. Next, we shouldn't compete. Forget the hare. All we have to do is just move. Third, we should not expect any particular result from our efforts. This means that if you try to attain enlightenment by doing zazen, your effort is misguided. It will make you lose your way. Soon you will start to look at yourself and say, "I can't attain enlightenment." Such thinking will exhaust you until you won't be able to do anything.

Just free yourself from any kind of label—both those you give yourself and those put on you by others. If you want to do zazen, all you have to do is sit down. If you compete with others, your zazen will become fearful and restless. Even if other people attain enlightenment, that's their story, not yours. Forget what others say or do and attend to your practice.

The last tie we need to sever in order to perfect the precepts is superstition. This is expressed in the precepts of taking refuge in the Buddha, the Dharma, and the Sangha, or the Triple Treasure. To take refuge is not about escaping the human world. True refuge is seeing the depth of human existence. True refuge is where everyone meets.

A buddha is any person who understands human life on the basis of impermanence and cause and effect. If you live like this, you are Buddha. Everyday life is difficult. We are loaded with preconceptions, prejudices, customs, and hereditary factors. This is why we have to come back to this moment and take refuge in living the life of a buddha. A buddha's efforts never cease.

Dharma is the teaching given by any person who understands the human world on the basis of impermanence and cause and effect. All we have to do is hook into this teaching and grow. To do this, however, we need help. We need the sangha.

The sangha is made up of those who come together to practice the Buddha's Way. Without this, Dharma teaching will not be transmitted to future generations. So all of us are needed to practice the Buddha's Way.

When we take up the Buddha's Way, the precepts are not seen as rules but as ways to manifest ourselves as buddhas. In our daily life, we must return to the precepts again and again. This effort is very important. It's the effort of simply walking forward, step-by-step, just like the tortoise.

_____ A painting of a rice cake

WHEN ZEN MASTER KYOGEN became a monk, his teacher asked him to say something about himself before his parents were born. He couldn't answer this question.

It is said he contemplated this question day after day for years, until, finally, he found the answer. He said, "Painting a rice cake doesn't satisfy hunger."

This saying is usually misunderstood, or it is understood only in a very narrow sense. So Dogen Zenji wrote about it to help us understand what it really means.

If you want to make a rice cake, you have to use rice, fire, firewood—many things. The same is true of nature. If you want to paint a rice cake, you have to use paint, a brush, and a canvas. Again, it takes many things. The same applies to becoming a buddha. A buddha is nothing but a painting of a rice cake, because a buddha is produced by the arousal of Bodhi Mind, practice, Enlightenment, and Nirvana. According to tradition, there are many kinds of buddhas, but they all paint their lives by arousing the Bodhi Mind, practice, Enlightenment, and Nirvana.

The same applies to human life. Human beings are produced by the five aggregates of form, feelings, perceptions, impulses, and consciousness—the five skandhas. But when we start to paint, many different kinds of pictures are produced—using our heredity, memories, emotions, and so on. So there are many kinds of human beings, but we all use the five aggregates to paint our lives.

But the real question is, How do we, as the painters of our lives, use our colors? Which colors do we choose? If we use the color called "this present moment," we can paint our life with it, but it's very narrow. If we use the colors of past and future, we can paint a broader picture of our life, which is a little better than just painting our life in the present only.

But still, if we paint just our life on the canvas, there is no warmth or compassion. We have disregarded others. So, naturally, the life we have painted for ourselves never settles down into peace and harmony. It's not really alive. It's cold and dead. It's not the fluidity of human life spoken of by the bodhisattvas.

So, how should we use the colors of our lives—the five skandhas as well as our past, present, and future? They must be intimately connected with each other. This is what the Buddha did—he painted the past, present, and future as a circle, not as something linear or as something composed of separate things.

The Buddha painted his life by using the colors of Bodhi Mind, practice, Enlightenment, and Nirvana. We must use these colors in harmony, not as separate things. In fact, they can't actually exist as separate things. Past, present, and future are never separate either. Within Bodhi Mind there is Nirvana; within Nirvana, Bodhi Mind can be found. This is the way the Buddha painted his life.

In this way, human life is nothing but the painting of a rice cake. And what is Buddhism? It, too, is nothing but the painting of a rice cake. The truth of human life is nothing but the painting of a rice cake, and Buddha's teachings are nothing but the painting of human life.

Any time we try to explain life, it's nothing but a painting. It's just thought. Concepts. Utter abstractions. These things will never satisfy our hunger. This is why human beings are always hungry. This hunger is pretty deep. It's not the usual hunger that we experience through our senses. This hunger is very profound—it's there before we're conscious of it. This is what the buddhas paint; this is what they try to draw to our attention. Whether we want this hunger or not, we are already hungry. Beyond any sense of good or bad, we are always hungry.

This hunger is what the Buddha called *dukkha*—suffering that comes from the depths of human life. Even before we are conscious of it, beyond our likes and dislikes, suffering is always there. It is very quiet, yet very dynamic. Whether we meet with success or failure, we can never be rid of it.

To produce a masterpiece, a painter can never find satisfaction. No matter what the painter accomplishes, there is still a deep hunger that encourages him to continue to paint. He can never stop. Though people appreciate his accomplishments, which benefit many, he is never satisfied. He just continues to paint.

But, in living his life, he can discover the flow of his effort. What makes it possible for him to continue? His hunger—his very deep suffering. But though it is suffering, it is also great encouragement. It nurtures his sensitivity to colors and the rhythms of nature. So, in a sense, it is not really suffering, because within it there is the very strong encouragement to live, to understand, to see, and to hear.

We can't escape hunger; we can't escape suffering. It is a truth of human life. But if we can understand this hunger, if we can see how deep our suffering is, then we can discover total freedom. Total freedom is found in realizing that there is nothing to satisfy. And this realization is found in the flow of life itself.

In Buddhism the painting of a rice cake that we see and experience is called a provisional being. Like so, the human life we can speak of is also a provisional existence. The moment we speak of it, it is separated from the whole of Reality. But the whole of Reality is all things—provisional being and original nature—coming together and working as One, right *now*, right *here*. This is True Reality.

Often, when people first learn of this basic teaching of the Buddha, they think it means that human life is not very important, that it is corrupt, or that it is on a lower level than the Buddha's life. This dualistic understanding is very common. But according to the Buddha's teaching, there is no separation between ordinary beings and buddhas. This "no separation" is beyond satisfaction or dissatisfaction. This is True Reality, and we can *see*, *hear*, and deal with it directly. But if we try to explain it in a word, such as "Emptiness," it is just an explanation. It is nothing but the painting of a rice cake, which never satisfies.

Human beings always want explanations, and we continually create them. But after all our explaining about skandhas, about past, present, and future, about the original nature of existence, what have we got? Just the painting of a rice cake. There is no way to conceptualize Truth. But is Truth separate from that painting of a rice cake? Separate from everyday life?

Zen master Kyogen finally gave a pretty deep answer to his teacher's question. What can we say about our original face? Although our commonsense understanding of the self is no understanding at all, there is something we can truly Know. How can we *see* what cannot be conceived?

The voice of Buddha

DOGEN ZENJI WROTE,

> The color of the peak,
> The sound of the valley,
> All are Shakyamuni's voice and figure.

Our experience is always *now*. It is pure motion with nothing moving. This activity penetrates every inch of the world—it is the world. And the world is nothing but conditioned elements. Things come into existence just like a chick that pecks at its shell from inside while its mother pecks from the outside. When the chick hatches, it appears different from its mother—but they are not exactly different. In the simultaneity of their activity, only one being really exists.

In the simultaneity of their activity, the many beings exist in just this way. That is why if you hear the voice of Buddha, you become Buddha. You already are Buddha. Like chick and mother hen, there is only one being that exists in Reality.

But how can you be Buddha? Just peck the shell and you will get a clue. If you peck the shell, something else pecks the shell, too. And then birth occurs. Not just your birth; the whole world comes into existence.

Who creates this birth? We don't know. You? No. Mother? No. The doctor? No. Nobody creates this birth. Real birth is produced by the activity of simultaneity. That is, your birth and the birth of the world occur simultaneously. This means becoming Buddha at hearing the voice of Buddha.

According to Buddhist philosophy, "One is all, and all is One." But how can we actualize the truth of this? Through the pure, undefiled practice of *shikantaza*, or *just sitting*—true zazen. True zazen is to tap the shell from inside, and while you tap, the shell is tapped from the outside—and then, Buddha happens. If you realize Buddha, simultaneously all beings—animate and inanimate—realize Buddha. All beings—even grasses, trees, and pebbles—necessarily attain the Way.

If we are caught by delusion, when we see trees, birds, and dogs, they remain trees, birds, and dogs—that is, they appear to be separate from us. We might even remind ourselves not to create these gaps between ourselves and other beings. But even while we talk about not creating gaps, we create gaps. If we truly create no gap, there is nothing to say. We just accept all beings as ourselves and live in peace and harmony. This is living a buddha's life. It is not so easy for us to do this. We can only do it if we *see* things as they are.

Even though we are not a buddha, we are already Buddha—we just don't recognize it. So, even though we don't recognize it, let's do the same things Buddha does. This is the meaning of the bodhisattva vow: though you haven't yet realized Buddhahood, you vow to do what Buddha does, which is to help all sentient beings.

To take care of other beings is to take care of your life in its totality. For instance, if you want to take care of tomorrow, take better care of today. Though tomorrow and today appear different, there is always some communication between them. This is the activity of simultaneity, which is very pure, clean, and undefiled. The activity of simultaneity is single-pointed concentration. To develop and use this kind of concentration is to bring all beings together, right now, right here, and to be one with them.

We all understand that time passes from today to tomorrow. But we don't understand at all that time also passes from today to yesterday. Actually, time passes away from *this moment* in all directions. As Dogen mentions, time also passes from today to today, because today is morning, afternoon, evening, and night. They seem separate, but in their simultaneity they're not.

By virtue of the activity of simultaneity, realization is manifested without hindrance. At the moment of realization—at the moment of Truth—before you are conscious of it, all beings penetrate you simultaneously. This is what Dogen calls walking in the mist. If you walk in the mist, before you are conscious of it, your clothes get wet. Here, walking means being one with the mist through the activity of simultaneity. And what is the mist? The whole world.

At the moment of actualization, each thing comes forward without opposing any other. All things work together in the whole fabric as one piece. But if you create a conceptual gap, you will create conflict.

To develop and deepen this kind of understanding, all you need to do is continually practice single-pointed concentration. Beyond thought, your body and mind are already right in the middle of dynamic activity. From the beginningless past, your life has been interpenetrated and interwoven with the lives of many beings. As Dogen put it, in penetrating one thing, you penetrate all things. This means, if you see one person's life, take care of it—not as one person, but as all beings. So one thing is not one thing. One thing is all things, manifested as one thing.

To penetrate one thing doesn't take away its original nature, nor does it set that one thing in relation to other things. If we truly penetrate one thing, we see no other. There is no comparing here.

This is not an abstract teaching. This teaching is actually very practical. It's something we have to do, day by day. For example, if you say, "I'm a Zen Buddhist," you might then compare yourself to Christians, Hindus, Jews, and others. It's natural to do this, but don't get bogged down by your comparisons. The point is, right in the middle of such discrimination, how can you settle yourself in peace and harmony? This is Zen practice.

But if you say, "I shouldn't compare," this is also not good. Comparisons are always going on in our minds. It's like in zazen when we think "Don't think." We immediately try not to think, but this is already thinking. When you allow penetration to be unhindered by penetration, one penetration is myriad penetrations. Total penetration is to walk in the mist until your clothes become completely wet—even before you're conscious of it.

If you are truly in single-pointed concentration, there is no gap between you and single-pointed concentration. Your mind is single-pointed concentration; your body is single-pointed concentration. But this doesn't mean your body disappears. It is only the conceptual frame, the idea of "my body," that disappears. This is not abstract. It is true reality, which you can taste. It's the true state of everything.

Basho's heart

THE ZEN POET BASHO WROTE:

Treading the mountain path,
The violets fill my heart
With indefinable gracefulness.

Though no one pays any attention to the violets along the path, they still bloom—quietly, beautifully, elegantly. To these flowers, Basho extends his warm heart.

If, unlike Basho, we see only the form of violets, we may think, "Why bloom here? Why don't you bloom in a beautiful garden, where people will pay attention to you?" But we have to see the violets as more than just material things. The violets also have power and life force. Set in the proper place, the material form of the violets works perfectly. The violets grow and bloom.

But where does this life force come from? Is it something flowers just have? If so, then where is it? Is it inside them, or outside them? We look, but we can't find it anywhere. Yet the flower blooms.

This power, this life force, is produced by many conditional factors coming together. Out of this, all of a sudden, a sentient being comes alive. It's like touching your skin: immediately a feeling goes through every cell, and the whole body comes alive.

If we look at violets with only our physical eyes, all we see is form. We don't pay any attention to the particular workings of the life force that makes a violet from what is not a violet. Where is the power that makes a flower blue or yellow, white or red? Where does the color come from? What makes its fragrance? We don't know. But if we put a flower in the proper place, it blooms and grows. The life force makes it come alive. We should know that, behind the form that we can see, there is a huge, unseen world at work.

Of course, the term *life force* is just a concept. But the actual life force is not a concept. It is nothing we can grasp. It's the activity that makes the material world come alive. This is why we must see deeply into the life of the violet. Through the material form of a violet, we can perceive the huge world at work behind what we usually see with our eyes.

The working of the violet is marvelous and complex. Its roots spread out underground, working around rocks and penetrating hard soil. It lives by means of very complicated procedures, yet it is never confused. It just grows, supported by both the material world and the force of life. The violet blooms as just a violet, with nothing to compare it to.

Basho is very sensitive to the beauty he sees. He shares the warmth of his heart with the violets of the mountain. His heart fills with indefinable gracefulness, because the violets are themselves indefinable gracefulness.

The eight wondrous places of the human world

ACCORDING TO BUDDHIST MYTHOLOGY, the human world has eight wondrous places that give us protection. The first is a place where everyone is illuminated by a golden light. This golden light supports all sentient beings and helps them to grow and mature under all circumstances. Consider your own life. For the past ten, twenty, thirty, or forty years, how many troubles have you experienced? Countless troubles. But still, you're alive. How? You don't know. But this is reality. You are a survivor. You have been protected and nurtured by many things—your parents, your teachers, your friends, and more. All this time, your life has been supported. You have been illumined by a golden light that constantly shines, and constantly helps you.

The second place is one in which you are immune to trouble. Of course, we all have troubles. But if you learn something from your troubles, then those troubles aren't exactly troubles. By realizing the true nature of trouble, trouble disappears. If you understand it properly, life really doesn't have trouble. Even though the human world is a place of trouble, it is also a place where all troubles disappear. This is why you have to take care of your troubles now. You can't escape them, but you can take care of them with wholeheartedness.

The third place is where you can awaken to Truth. There are people in the world who have awakened, and they can help you. So it is possible to open your heart and find a great person who can help you. But you have to find such a person; don't expect the person to come looking for you.

The fourth place is one in which you can practice the bodhisattva's six perfections: giving, morality, patience, effort, imperturbability, and wisdom. The practice of giving is not a matter of having no desires but of keeping your balance within the realm of desire. This is difficult, but you can learn it. The practice of morality comes with the full understanding that you can't live alone and so you must learn to be considerate of others. Patience comes with learning to look with openmindedness beyond what is unpleasant. To make every possible effort to live with all sentient beings is to practice imperturbability. As long as you live with other beings, you must make your mind calm and see the total picture of human life—both your life and the lives of others. In this way you can experience wisdom—deep insight into the true nature of all living beings.

The fifth wondrous place of the human world is where life is lived as an art. Here the beauty of one's life is manifested, both physically and mentally, and here we can learn what the human world actually is.

Three more places give us protection. In one you can learn innumerable things beyond what you already know. In the next, people in all kinds of professions—political leaders, artists, physicians, philosophers, psychologists, ministers, and priests—can gather to share what they do and to discuss how they can work with each other. Finally, there is a place through which all the majestic heavens pass. This is where all the pure lands of the buddhas appear.

The human world is not a terrible place. It is a pure place that manifests beauty. Wherever you may be in this world, you can take care of your life by letting the beautiful flower of your life force bloom.

Walking alone, as all beings

THERE ARE TWO DISCOURSES on the sangha by the Buddha that appear to be contradictory. In one he speaks of the virtues of living in solitude. In the other he says we should find a wise and good friend with whom we can walk through life. But these teachings aren't actually contradictory. Both refer to the spirit of self-discovery, of coming to the realization that you live with all beings and that your life is inseparable from those of others.

To live in solitude is to live with the understanding that there is nothing to depend on. Ordinarily this realization means great suffering for us because, according to our usual sense of things, we try to depend on things outside ourselves that we can hold fast to. But when viewed more deeply, we can see that suffering occurs only because we see ourselves as separate in the first place.

Strictly speaking, no matter what situation you are in, happy or sad, you live alone, and your practice is to walk steadily and alone. Most people read this teaching in a pessimistic way, but it is not a pessimistic or negative way of life at all. If we understand it properly, it is actually very positive.

The Buddha also taught that if you come across a true friend—one who is noble, fearless, thoughtful, and wise—then walk with that friend in peace. If you find such a friend, you can walk together for life. But don't be too eager to find such a friend. If you become greedy for such a friend, you will be disappointed, and you will not be able to live in peace and harmony with others.

Learning to live alone means that, whatever the situation, you have to live quietly. All you have to do is just walk, step-by-step. It's not so easy, but it's very important for us. And if we are not too greedy, the good friend will appear.

In ancient times in India, people would look to find such a good friend meditating in the forest. If they found such a person, they would sit with him. This is how it was with Buddha. As people began to gather around him, he called them *shravakas*, which means "listeners." The relationship between the Buddha and those who came to listen to his teaching was not like that of a boss and an employee or a parent and child. It was more like that of a master and an apprentice. If you go to see and listen to such a wise friend, you are not a student, exactly; you are just a listener. The idea of being called a student came about in a later age.

At the time of the Buddha, there were four castes of people, and depending on caste, there were many formal rules for how people should address one another. But the Buddha was beyond classifying or discriminating among people. He used the same kind, gentle, and polite form of expression to address everyone, no matter what the station. He only said, "Welcome." That's it. People didn't go through any particular ceremony that certified them as followers of the Buddha. They just received this simple greeting. This is the origin of the sangha.

In Sanskrit the term *sangha* literally means "group." It was used to refer to religious groups as well as political groups. When the Buddha visited different regions, the people would gather together to listen to his teaching and to practice together. Then, after he left, they would settle into small groups or take up traveling.

Today, how do we find a wise friend? I don't know. There is no particular pattern. But even though you might not find such a good friend in this world, still you can find a good friend in the example of the Buddha. And if you do come across such a friend, walk with him. Just remember, if this person is a good friend for you, he is also a good friend for others, so don't attach too strongly to him.

You can feel something from such persons as you walk with them. And remember, though they are human beings living now, through them you can meet the Buddha. And through the Buddha, you can see such a good, pure friend.

Make yourself at home

IN HIS *Instructions for the Cook*, Dogen Zenji wrote:

> Put those things that naturally go on a high place onto a high place, and those that would be most stable on a low place onto a low place; things that naturally belong on a low place find their greatest stability there.

Dogen is not talking about hierarchy here. He's simply saying that if you put a cup on a high shelf it can easily break if it drops to the floor. If you put it on a lower shelf, it's safer. In other words, you have to understand, as clearly as you can, the life of the cup. You have to understand what a cup is, what a knife is, what a fork is. You have to understand the life of each thing with compassion, kindness, friendliness, and consideration. Although Dogen presents this as advice to the chief cook, it is really instruction for us all about how to live. Without intruding or being overbearing, we must put ourselves in the place of others and learn to deal with them as they are.

Once we know the life of the spoon or the cup, it's very clear where they should go. But we should understand that their place is never separate from us. Their place, like ours, is the universal place in which all sentient beings are perfectly situated. If we think in terms of hierarchy, then we will see everything as existing separate from us. For example, through our conceptual understanding, we will see a tree as being completely different from ourselves. But the tree actually exists beyond our conceptual understanding. It exists in that universal place of equality with all beings.

When you sit in zazen, the tree has already returned home and sits with you in peace and harmony. At this time, the tree finds its own place, the place where it exists naturally. But if you think the tree is really separate from you, then the tree becomes just a concept.

Flowers bloom in spring, not in winter. But whatever the season, flowers become flowers as they are, and trees become trees as they are. This is important for us to understand. When a flower becomes a flower as it is, it teaches us about its actual existence. When a tree becomes a tree as it is, it creates a wonderful world that is rich and generous. When we allow the tree to become a tree as it is, we have close and intimate communication with it. Why? Because it is just there, creating a wonderful space where everyone can feel relief.

If we just think in our ordinary, dualistic way, we can't find such a space. If we only study trees biologically and physically, as though they are objects separate from us, we then will have no true understanding of what a tree is. We don't understand that when we make it an object, we kill the life of the tree.

The result of viewing everything in this way is that each thing appears to be a separate entity. In other words, the moment you say "Katagiri," Katagiri is separate from you. We never question this. We say, "Of course, this is how it is. Katagiri *is* separate from me." But strictly speaking, it's not so. If you live in that way, you will never experience this warm and majestic space of True Reality. You will create a very cold space.

You have to return home and sit in peace and harmony. This means placing the tree just where it ought to be to express its life as a tree, placing the cup just where it ought to be to express its life as a cup, placing the fork just where it ought to be to express its life as a fork. If you leave the fork on the floor, you kill the life of the fork.

As chief cook, you have to deal with forks, vegetables, pans, and so on, placing them where they ought to be. The best way to take care of your objects is for you, the subject, to just merge with them. When you extend your life to them, you give them the chance to extend their lives to you. This creates a soft and wonderful space through which you all communicate. This magnanimous space is Buddha's world.

When we invite guests to our home, we always say, "Please make yourself at home." We want them to feel comfort and acceptance. We want them to express themselves as they are and with enjoyment. But out in the world, where is the place where you feel at home? If you regard the human world with just the intellect, there is no place where you can make yourself at home. With your ordinary understanding, everything remains apart from you, and the things around you don't speak to you. So it doesn't seem to matter what you do with the things around you.

But when things are placed where they ought to be—that is, if you just allow them to be what they are—they very naturally start to talk with you. You feel at home in the wonderful space you have allowed to happen around you. This is what Dogen is saying to us.

> Both day and night, allow all things to come into and reside within your mind. Allow your mind and all things to function together as a whole.

We can't have close communication with our objects if they appear as separate beings. We should move toward them. In other words, allow things to come up to you and reside within your mind. This is throwing yourself into the home of Buddha. Buddha's home is where all objects are placed just as they are. It's the natural world we find around us. Just return home and reside there in peace and harmony.

If you want to be a mountaineer, you have to climb the mountain day by day, throwing yourself into the life of the mountain. The real life of the mountain is the total picture of the mountain, where all things—clouds, sky, birds, and all sentient beings—appear as they are. It's the whole universe. To truly climb the mountain is to communicate with all beings.

It is risky to climb a mountain, so, intellectually, we don't understand why we love mountains so much. But we like the richness, the softness, the calm majesty that allows us to return home and sit in peace and harmony with the life of the mountain.

The mountain's true life is the life of birds and pebbles, trees and rivers—the same life as yours. To learn this just throw yourself into Buddha's home. As Dogen said, day and night, allow all things to come and reside with your heart and mind, and they will function together as a whole. All things will open up and start to talk with you. This wonderful feeling is experienced beyond ideas and thoughts.

In his essay "Bendowa," Dogen expressed the same thing in a different way. He wrote:

> The sound that issues from the striking of Emptiness is an endless and wondrous voice that resounds before and after the fall of the hammer.

We're always striking Emptiness, but we don't realize it. We ignore Emptiness. We deal with things dualistically. The problem is that, whether we're conscious of it or not, we believe being caught up in dualism is the only true way to live. But according to Dogen, the sound that issues from striking Emptiness is the universal marketplace, where everything is situated just where it ought to be. It is that place where all things exist as they are: where red flowers are red, green willows are green, and Katagiri is Katagiri. To abide in this place is wisdom.

Basho wrote that we can create a haiku as soon as we can *see* the light each object emits. Basho wasn't talking about a halo, of course. He means you should *see* more than what you see with just your naked eyes. Light here refers to *seeing* the accuracy of the manifestation of existence—*seeing* that you, the flower, the trees, and all of nature are perfectly situated in the universal marketplace. We can't get an idea of it. Nevertheless, we can *see* that all things already exist in this way.

This light is the accuracy with which a flower becomes what it is. It doesn't come from any place in particular; it comes from the whole universe. When we truly sit in zazen, we, too, manifest our own existence with accuracy. But if we sit as we usually do, with our bodies and minds moving and looking about, the accuracy of our existence doesn't show. We sit as if removed from ourselves. If you can truly sit *here*, you will create a soft, magnanimous place, and people will feel comfort and acceptance just from observing your sitting.

The voiceless voice

IF WE OBSERVE THE HUMAN WORLD closely, we can hear a very deep sound. It is a kind of voice, yet it is voiceless. If we are very quiet, we can hear this voiceless voice in the bottom of the human heart. Wherever you may be, whatever you experience, if you are present, you will immediately hear it. But you can't hear it with your ears. Does it express pleasure? Is it sad? Is it good? You can't evaluate it. It is just there; and you are there, too. Whether you are in the middle of success or failure, your life cries.

There is a famous bodhisattva named Avalokiteshvara, whose name means "regarder of the cries of the world." Avalokiteshvara is all of us, but not any one of us in particular. We are all present in the middle of the human world at once, in the middle of good, bad, suffering, pleasure, emptiness, and kindness. So the Regarder of the Cries of the World never focuses on a particular person or situation. Nor does she pray for human desire to be satisfied. Avalokiteshvara's concerns are always focused on us all.

We have to listen for the voice that she hears deep within us—the cries of the world. It is the basis of our existence. Though we try to explain it psychologically or philosophically, all explanations are secondary. The immediate Reality is that, day by day, we are here, we are present. And so, with our whole body and mind, we have to hear the voiceless voice, the cryless cry, which comes from very deep within the human world. To hear it, all we have to do is be present.

Even now you are suffering. But what can you say about your suffering? There is nothing to pin down, nothing to say. The voiceless voice, which comes from the depths of human life, can't be measured. Yet it is always there. It is what you actually experience. Somehow—in a word, through your body, with your mind—you must express it.

If you just sit down in the midst of this quiet suffering, you become Avalokiteshvara, and you can listen to the voiceless voice of the world. You can open yourself to whatever situation you may be in. It's no use saying that the suffering out there in the world is foreign, that it doesn't belong to you. You have to take care of it every day, because it has already appeared. Just keep yourself open to it. This is true compassion.

Compassion is always with us, but ordinarily we let our heads come first. We evaluate each situation, we single out certain people, talk about them, put them down, and so forth. But though we like to talk about others, though it seems to make us feel good, this is not the way out of our suffering. If we would deal with our suffering, we can't talk about particular people. Actual suffering—the voiceless voice of the world— does not belong to any particular person. While the world of human suffering is infinite, particular people are not infinite.

To regard the cries of the world, we have to be open to all situations. We can't put a price on our life or on the lives of others. We have to see our life and the lives of others in a completely different kind of world than our usual world of this and that. Otherwise, we will never understand Reality in its fullness. In other words, do your best without looking around. Just concentrate on what needs to be done.

PART TWO

Egolessness

Where are you now?

DOGEN ZENJI COMPARED OUR LIFE to rowing a boat. Rowing a boat means that you are onboard the boat. It is the place where you are. This is very important, but most people don't pay attention to it. What people are most interested in is the rowing of the boat. They focus only on their efforts, goals, and abilities, and completely forget about where they are.

The place where you are is not just your place. If you actually see where you are, you will see that you are one with the boat, the water, the near shore, and the far shore. You are one with the sky, the birds, and the motion of the boat. In other words, you, the boat, the water, the near and far shores, and the sky are all moving together. Where you are is completely beyond your control. And yet you still have to row the boat.

If you think that you can accomplish everything just by your own effort, you are ignoring the fact that you're already on the boat with all beings. You are all moving along together. If you believe that everything you need to do can be done just by personal efforts, you will eventually fall into desperation, because in time you will find a situation where your effort alone is not enough. Then you might think of yourself as a failure. This is a common feeling people get when they ignore the most important place, the place where they actually are.

We ignore the boat, this shore, the other shore, and all sentient beings in the belief that we can do everything through our own power. But it's impossible. In fact, you can't touch anything Real by just your own effort. If you try to touch what is Real, immediately you fall into delusion. This is the human situation.

In San Francisco in the 1960s there were hippies everywhere. I met many who came to the Zen center, but I also met them on the streetcars. That's where I asked one of them, "Where are you going?" He said, "I don't know. Ask the streetcar."

That was the usual understanding of Zen in those days. It's pretty nice, don't you think? Nice and soft, like a downy cushion. But it's really a big misunderstanding. It is to forget that you are already in the water and that you have to row the boat. If you don't know where you're headed, and you just depend on the boat, you are completely confused.

Dogen's message is very important for us. It is really a great opportunity to see human life from a broader perspective. This is the heart of our practice, to see our lives together with all beings.

Throw yourself away

IN LEARNING WHO AND WHAT you are, you realize how your ego-consciousness corroborates what you are doing. Ego-consciousness appears on the surface of your daily life as "Yes, I am doing zazen" or "I want to do zazen," and so forth.

Ego-consciousness may seem to be strong, but it is actually very weak. It is always going to the right, going to the left—just like a pendulum. Finally, however, your ego-consciousness realizes that there is nothing to say. At that time, in the realm of nothing to say, you will reach an impasse, a terminating abode. As long as you try to figure out what to do, the situation will get worse.

When this happens, just sit down. To come to an impasse is to do zazen. To do zazen is to have nothing to say about this impasse. To have nothing to say about this impasse means your body and mind have become the impasse. Just sit down and take a long, deep breath. That's all we have to do.

To just sit means not to expect anything from this impasse. Just be one with the impasse. Throw away even the idea of an impasse. Zazen is not a means to an end or an escape or the promise of reward. Neither is it a matter of figuring out the meaning of the impasse. Zazen is to return to the original nature of the self based on emptiness. At that time, you have a great chance to turn around completely.

If you deeply understand human life, there is nothing to say. In other words, the original nature of the self is not some idea in your mind. True self manifests itself in daily life. How can we manifest this original self? With full concentration and no attachment. Another word for no attachment is wisdom—deep knowledge that keeps your life balanced in peace and harmony. Full concentration means to merge with zazen when you do zazen, to merge with bowing when you bow, and so forth.

To merge with zazen is not so easy, It requires strong determination. In other words, you have to completely throw yourself away in zazen. Dogen Zenji tells us to throw away good and bad, right and wrong—to have no designs on becoming enlightened. When you become one with zazen, through and through, there is no attachment. This is peaceful, harmonious mind.

This must be your aim, otherwise you won't experience zazen as it really is. Of course, many things and ideas come up in zazen, but those things and ideas are just bubbles. The moment you meddle with them, you immediately provoke a sense of irritation, hatred, depression, and so forth. Oneness with zazen implies no meddling. It means no idea of practice and no idea of practicer. If you truly do zazen, very naturally, the idea of a practicer and the idea of zazen will drop off. Then you will be free of zazen.

Opening your heart

FOR ANYONE LIVING A SPIRITUAL LIFE, the most important practice is openheartedness. But dealing with life with compassion and kindness is not easy. We tend to live in terms of "me." But if you're interested in the spiritual life, you will have to consider more than just yourself.

All religions emphasize the importance of openness of heart. But very few of us actually practice it in our daily lives. So day after day, year after year, century after century, wise people point this out to us. They know how egotistical we are. But even one person practicing love and compassion is a great source of peace in the world.

Whatever the future brings, we have to continue to seek a world based on the practice of openness of heart. Perfect openness of heart brings into life flexibility, tenderness, and magnanimity. This can't be fully explained conceptually. You can't put your finger on it, but you can feel it. To live this way is what you're really looking for.

Usually we live our lives only in terms of the world we can see. When we do, we emphasize ourselves. We place the "I" first. Even when we take up the spiritual life, we place the "I" first. In other words, we pull everything down to the level of our personal views and feelings. We never forget ourselves. This is why, at bottom, we're often irritated or uneasy. And the more we place the "I" first, the more irritation, uneasiness, suffering, and fear we feel.

What we tend to ignore is the world that sees us. This is not the world you think you see or hear. Nevertheless, you are supported by this world. It is actually the world as it is *before* you are conscious of it—before you form some idea about it. If you emphasize yourself, you will completely forget this world that sees, holds, and sustains you.

For instance, since I'm the head of a Zen group, even though my life is my life, my life is not really my life. My life is really the life of all of the group. So, very naturally, even though I don't like it, we set up a schedule for zazen, and lectures, and retreats, and so forth—and I have to follow it. In other words, the group has set me in a certain way of life. In terms of my ego, I don't like it. I'd rather do just what I want to do, and not always follow the schedule.

We all feel this way from time to time. We say, "Don't tell me what I should do!" But we can't take care of our lives very well just based on our personal preferences. There's a big world that sees you. You can't ignore this world. So, even though I might not like it sometimes, the group provides me with this great opportunity to sit zazen. So when the opportunity appears, I feel grateful that I can sit zazen with all beings.

We all have memories and habits and patterns in our lives, and sometimes, even though we feel good, they don't allow us to open our hearts. Intellectually we know we should, but emotionally it seems like we can't. Still, you can do it. Strictly speaking, openness of heart is beyond all speculation. It is the total picture of your life as you live it from day to day.

If you want to practice compassion, you must accept simultaneously the world you see and the world that sees you. You can't judge your life just in terms of what you can see—that is, from your ego-centered perspective. You must practice patience, calmness of mind, and mindfulness. If you don't confine yourself to just your own view of things, these come up naturally. When you just sit down in zazen, you can feel something. Even though you don't know what it is, it just arises, right here, right now.

Compassion is like springwater under the ground. Your life is like a pipe that can tap into that underground spring. When you tap into it, water immediately comes up. So drive your pipe into the ground. Tap into the water of compassion. We can't conceive of what real compassion and openness of heart are, but if you tap into them, you can feel them. If you learn to deal with your life with compassion, magnanimity, and flexibility, you will become very tender, generous, and kind. This is all that is necessary.

We do not need an explanation. No matter how long we ask about why we are so egoistic, we will never find a clear answer. Nevertheless, right in the middle of this "no answer," your life goes on. Even though we don't understand, we can all take a deep breath. We can all practice forgetting ourselves. Forgetting yourself does not mean destroying yourself. Forgetting yourself is just to see yourself from a different angle: the way the world sees you. Then you will see not just your little ego self but your true self, your big self, which includes all beings.

When I was fourteen years old my mother died. The world seemed completely dark. I felt there was no hope for me. Day after day, I cried in my bed. It seemed that the more I cried, the more I tried to reach for her, the further from me she became. So I cried even more. I cried constantly. But, all of a sudden, I stopped crying. I felt my mother had come into my heart. I can't explain it in words. But there was no longer any separation between me and my mother. She was in my heart.

This goes for you, too. There is you and then there is the world. If there is even a small gap between them, we fill it with thought. As long as we create this gap, we will never understand. But in Truth, there is no gap between you and the world. To become one with your object is true openness of heart. This is why we do zazen.

using the selfish self

ZAZEN IS GOOD PRACTICE FOR US. We can call it perfume, because it scents our life. Of course, whatever we practice scents our life. If, for example, you become an army officer, your life becomes very armylike. Even when you wear normal clothes, people can still smell your army clothes. Because I am a Zen priest from Japan, even when I wear Western clothes, people still smell the "monk" on me. I cannot escape.

We often don't like the smells that perfume the air around us, so we resist them. We say we want to be free. But the kind of freedom that includes such resistance is questionable. True freedom is not found in the air that surrounds you. You find it by noticing how you resist the perfume of others and then, moment to moment, you let yourself breathe whatever perfume fills the air.

We sometimes have the idea that if we don't think of ourselves first, we will fall behind. But the more we try to get ahead, the more exhausted we become. We cannot escape self-centered ideas. So instead of denying or destroying the self, we must ask, how can we use our selfish self in a simple, practical way? To use this selfish self compassionately is the practice of Zen Buddhism. Compassion is like springwater coming up from the ground, and it can be used to sustain everyone.

But even if we learn to use our life for all sentient beings, we may still have a sense of selfishness: "I am using my selfishness for everyone. I am saving all sentient beings." It's better to just help others without leaving any trace. There's no reason to think, "I am doing this for others."

Our little self is very selfish. You have to understand, through and through, how strongly you love your little self. To do this, however, the self you must realize is not this small self. It is your true self, which is actually the same as the true self of others. In other words, you have to extend your idea of self to include everyone and everything.

We often try to protect ourselves by sacrificing someone else. But the best way of protecting yourself doesn't entail benefiting at the expense of others. The best way is to work in close cooperation with others. This is also how you establish true self. But you will not establish true self if you try to share your life with others while still holding only to your own view.

For instance, consider a baby and its mother. The baby offers no words. She doesn't say, "I am hungry," "I am sleepy," "I have a stomachache." She doesn't say anything. She just cries. Yet, behind her crying, her mother understands what she wants. At that time she can establish the self that is exactly the same as that of others. What is the true self of the mother? Of the baby? They are exactly the same.

When you love someone, what can you say about it? Even though you say nothing, both of you understand pretty well. This is cooperation; this is living together as one. If you always have to explain how much you love someone, it will create a lot of creaking noises between you. Though you try to cooperate, your interaction becomes rigid. If neither party understands what is unexplainable regarding the other, life will not go smoothly. We have to understand others even when they don't say anything about their needs and wants. Only then can you cooperate—just like a baby and its mother.

Egolessness

IMPERMANENCE, THE FACT THAT everything is constantly changing, is one of Buddha's main teachings. It's not so easy to stand up in a world of constant change. Nothing lasts—not our bodies, not our minds, not our likes or our dislikes. If this is true, how should we live? In egolessness.

Egolessness is not about destroying or ignoring the subjective side of life. It means noticing that subjectivity is intimately related to what appears "out there." In other words, both the subject, "me," and the object, "that," exist together, beyond our likes and dislikes. The important point, then, is how to exist within this realm that comprises both subject and object. In other words, how can we live in peace and harmony? Dealing with this question is the main purpose of Buddhism.

Usually we just see things from our own point of view, according to our preconceptions, emotions, and preferences. We then try to manipulate and control the things that we see. But if we would live in peace and harmony, we must first handle things—this book, our clothes, our shoes—without killing them. Whatever feelings we have, we must take care of the objects and situations we face with a calm, generous, magnanimous mind.

If you bring in your personal point of view, even slightly, you immediately create a gap. This gap is hatred, aversion, anger. Suddenly life becomes pretty hard for us.

The world is completely beyond our likes and dislikes. All things work together as a dynamic whole. Because of impermanence, of thoroughgoing change, there is nothing to hold on to. In Buddhism we say everything is empty. Emptiness is just constant change. But don't think you can understand emptiness with concepts. There is no way to grasp it.

The depth of human life is ungraspable. In Buddhism, wisdom means penetrating this depth directly. Seeing the ultimate nature of existence, which is emptiness, you naturally begin to practice egolessness. Without creating any gaps between subject and object, you handle your life as both subject and object. In this complete and refined state of human activity, subject and object become one.

The face of emptiness

To RECEIVE WITH A GENEROUS MIND is to receive with no sense that things are either defiled or immaculate. It's to accept happiness within sickness, wealth within poverty, beauty within ugliness, and to realize that sickness is within happiness, poverty is within wealth, and ugliness is within beauty. To receive with a generous mind is to have no sense of ego, of self.

If there is a sense of ego—even a small sense of ego—there is some separation between you and your situation. So, if you are sick, you will hate your sickness, and you will complain about it. We all want to be free of suffering, of course, but we ignore how much we suffer because we tenaciously hold to our sense of self. Because we don't really know how to satisfy or protect this self, we suffer. We hate our predicament, because we don't know how to make a life based in suffering free from suffering.

Usually we ignore the reality of our life. We just assume that life is not suffering. We don't recognize that we have a problem, let alone contemplate that our problem is wholly within our own mind. We don't actually attend to what we face right here. Instead, our minds wander—to the right, to the left—until, finally, we suffer. We suffer because we always try to handle our immediate problem as though it were apart from us, as though it were "out there."

For instance, a Zen student approached his teacher. "I have a problem," he said. "I would like to start a business but, unfortunately, I don't have any money. What shall I do?"

"That's simple," said the Zen master. "Why don't you stop thinking about starting a business?"

"But I want to have a business."

"How can you without money?"

"That's why I'm suffering," said the student.

"I can't take away your suffering," said the master. "But who creates this suffering?"

If we are going to take care of our suffering, we have to Know the true face of Reality. For this, we must deepen our lives. We need wisdom. This wisdom is a function of the human heart and mind. It is our innate capacity to see beyond the dualistic world of greed and anger, to where we may learn to live in peace and harmony with all beings. This is not to escape the dualistic world. It is to take care of the dualistic world.

To do this, you must first calm your mind. For this, zazen works pretty well. But still, there's confusion. So we also need to study the Buddhist precepts. And we need to see what the Real face of existence actually is.

The true nature of existence is constant change. Since everything exists in the stream of time, nothing persists even for a moment. This means that all things are empty of an abiding self. In Zen we speak of two degrees of Emptiness. The first is seeing directly that everything is impermanent and that our lives are based in transiency. By closely studying this—which is our actual experience—we can actually lose our sense of ego. The second degree is experiencing Emptiness as the actual absence of our own being.

The true religious life must be free of any sense of self. Then the religious life is not just a religious life, because it extends to every aspect of human life.

For example, if you want to be a dancer, just do what you need to do without being obsessed by fame or criticism, praise or blame, success or failure. This is to deeply understand Emptiness. It is to experience the absence of your own being. This is to really become a dancer. Then, if fame appears, you don't depend on it. It's easy to become infatuated with fame, but if you do, you will stumble over it. One moment people may applaud you; in the next moment they may forget all about you. When we try to find happiness or stability in something outside, we are always uneasy. There is nothing out there to depend on.

The absence of our own being is the face of Emptiness. Emptiness is not produced nor is it stopped; it does not appear nor does it disappear. In experiencing the absence of our being, we become fully alive, for we are not dependent on things. This is to be free from suffering.

This is why we must do zazen without expecting any kind of reward. This is most important. If you miss this point, your zazen will be just like everything else you do. It will be the kind of meditation you find in pop psychology. In zazen you just do it. There is nothing to depend on.

But we always try to get something from zazen. Sometimes we might talk about how wonderful zazen is, how it makes our life better. This is not zazen. It is dissatisfaction, longing, and instability of mind. We are still depending on something. Consciously or unconsciously, we depend on things as if they had substance.

Even though I tell you Buddha is not something divine, you still conjure up a sense of divinity. Then you begin to feel you can depend on it. So I explain that Buddha is thoroughgoing change, or Emptiness, but still you don't believe me. Then I tell you that you are Buddha, so there is nothing for you to depend on. You don't believe this either. You don't take to heart what Buddha's teaching points out to you.

Consciously or unconsciously, we put something out there that makes us feel dependent. This is a big problem. It might seem to be good to be infatuated by some wonderful, spiritual experience, but it's not so good. It interrupts life—your life and the life of society.

So without asking for anything, expecting anything, or depending on anything, just do zazen. Then your life will become really alive.

Knowing the world
_____ before you measure it

To PRACTICE DEEPLY IS TO OBSERVE closely the Emptiness of existence. Unfortunately, when we use the term *observe*, the idea of an observer comes up immediately. You, the subject, come along with the object you are observing. For example, right now I'm looking at the tape recorder that's recording my talk. But the tape recorder I observe is not the tape recorder as it is—it is the tape recorder being observed by me.

Any object you study is measured by your own yardstick. So any absolutes you observe are not really Absolute. It is just stuff you have measured in relation to other things. To each thing you observe you bring your knowledge, your education, your past, your customs, your heredity. This is why we can all look at the same things but see them in different ways. This is our usual human experience.

But to approach the spiritual life like this is very dangerous. The point of the spiritual life is to realize Truth. But you will never understand the spiritual life, or realize Truth, if you measure it by your own yardstick.

Many religions tell us that if we are to embark upon the spiritual life, we must become like babies. This is not something we should take literally. What it means is that we must become egoless.

In his poem "Trusting the Heart-mind," Seng-ts'an, the third patriarch of Zen in China, tells us, "The Great Way knows no difficulties except that it refuses to hold preferences." To hold no preferences is to know the real meaning of Absolute, which is the world as it is *before* you measure it. What you measure and understand by your yardstick can sometimes make you feel pretty secure. You might say, "Oh, I understand the absolute," but this is not real understanding. What you understand is not the real Absolute; it is only some relative idea. Whatever you can measure by your yardstick is always very shaky.

If you want to know the real Absolute, you have to observe that everything is constantly moving and never stopping. Everything is constant change. This includes your eyes, your ears, your nose, and every pore of your body. Physically and mentally, all is constant motion. *This* is Absolute.

All things come together in a single event called "this moment." Right now, "this moment" appears, but we don't know what will happen next. When you see something moving, there's *only* movement. You cannot measure this total movement. All you can do is observe it directly and participate in it completely. This is to truly know total movement as total movement.

Actually, the idea of *your* participation is highly questionable. If you ask, "How can I participate in total movement?" the total movement you speak of is merely something measured by your yardstick. It is just an object relative to you, the subject.

Although "Trusting the Heart-mind" says that the Great Way—Truth, Reality, the Absolute—knows no difficulties, but only refuses to make preferences, this doesn't mean we should wipe away our preferences in order to know the Great Way. You will never succeed in doing that. To refuse to make preferences simply means to know the world as it is, *before* you measure it. For instance, we say we want peace and harmony, but what do peace and harmony mean, particularly in a world filled with terrifying new weapons? We can easily get lost in trying to figure out an answer to this problem. But real peace and harmony are very simple. Wherever you go, you can immediately practice them, because real peace and harmony are already in the world. Before you attempt to measure them, they are there.

The Great Way refers to our true heart. Our true heart knows no difficulties. Our true heart refuses to make preferences. Thus, when you sit down, just sit down. It's a very simple practice. To truly sit down is to sit down in the realm of total movement, to sit along with time and place and causes and conditions.

When you just sit down, real peace immediately appears. *Before* any object called "peace" appears, peace appears. So there is no room even to discuss peace. If you truly want peace, be peace, right now. Peace is not simply about keeping away from weapons. Real peace is to be peace now—immediately—in this moment.

People naturally sense this. Nevertheless, we try to make peace fit with our yardstick. Then when we can't seem to find peace, we get confused and frustrated. If we truly want peace, we must stop trying to measure it.

If we take hold of something that has a particular form, saying, "Yes, this is it! This is the truth!" we have then made Truth merely an idea. Soon we begin to discuss it and weigh it. But no matter how long we discuss such things, we will never find solutions to any of our questions. In time we will discover our idea doesn't always work. It's just relative.

Our problem is that we believe our relative truths are Absolute. This is why we are always fighting each other. We always try to get everything into our hands. We ignore the fact that whatever we can get into our hands is only what we have been able to measure by our yardstick. You can't possess Absolute as a form; you can't hold it in your hand. It is before any form appears. When we try to speak of it, naturally, negative terms appear.

People sometimes misunderstand Buddhism because it often uses expressions like no eyes, no ears, no nose, no heart, no mind, no self, no consciousness, and so forth. Sometimes they think Buddhism is nihilistic. But Buddhism is not nihilistic. It is not about the destruction of existence. It is about *seeing* the world before we measure it.

There is nothing to pin down because the reality we are living is constantly changing. Yet, while there's nothing to pin down, nothing to hold in our hand, still we have the sense of "I am here." And then we take hold of that idea. This is why everyone is confused.

There are Zen stories about a mountain named Egolessness. On this mountain there is a wonderful tree named Great Enlightenment. When you eat the fruit of this tree, you experience great spiritual excitement. People are very interested in such stories because they want to have some great, spiritual experience. They want to fly and go to paradise where there is no suffering.

Unfortunately, these people have no idea where this tree is. They don't even know where the mountain is. So they start checking every tree they come to, eating the fruit of each. Sometimes the fruit makes them feel dizzy; sometimes they lose their appetite. Still, they work very hard searching for the fruit of their dreams. In fact, their search is not even that hard for them, because they expect great things. Finally, the stories tell us, one person found what he thought was the enlightenment tree. When he ate its fruit, he experienced wonderful things. But his so-called enlightenment was just plain selfishness.

All of us are interested in looking for the enlightenment tree. Our problem is that we don't look for it on the mountain of egolessness. What we don't understand is that self-awakening must coincide with other-awakening. In other words, if we would awaken, we must help others to awaken.

Generally we approach practice with our eyes just on our own awakening. But this is to misunderstand practice. There *is* no self-awakening unless it is supported by other-awakening. The idea of awakening by oneself doesn't make sense. In fact, if, in your practice, you emphasize yourself, self-awakening doesn't happen. True practice can't take place without others.

To awaken others is to awaken one's self simultaneously. This is why we emphasize helping others first. This is how we can really help ourselves. So, instead of searching and scavenging for enlightenment, you need to ask yourself what truth you seek. What is your true heart?

We don't understand that the real bedrock of existence is pure motion. There is nothing to hold on to, nothing we can claim for ourselves. All we really have to do is just be here, and in that way we will learn what the world is before we measure it. Even though you don't understand what goes on before you measure it, just be here in peace. Just become peace. This is our practice.

To realize a buddha's life

THE HIGHEST LEVEL of human life is not to be found within our commonsense understanding of things. Still, we cannot ignore or escape these views. So we have to understand our commonsense ideas thoroughly, and then we must go beyond them.

To go beyond ordinary thought is to truly understand. If you just stay with your usual understanding of things, you will be like the frog that only swims in his small pond. Staying just within your little territory, you will never know anything about the larger world in which you live. You have to jump into the ocean. Then you can understand your small world for what it is. To jump into the ocean is to seek a buddha's life, the highest level of human life.

When we begin the quest for the highest level of human life, it doesn't feel good. But you have to leave behind any egoistic sense that you may have. Just study the life and work of the masters and practice. That's all you have to do, regardless of whether you like it or not.

Immediately we protest and say, "No! No, I can't do it! It's not human!" But this is because we see our lives in terms of common sense. We are always immersed in the world of our desires. But in order for us to understand our desires, both intellectual and physical, deeply, we have to go beyond them, even though we might not like it at the time.

In Minnesota, where I live, it can be very cold in the morning in April. But by eight o'clock, if you stand in the sun, you can feel pretty warm, even though it's still cold. Cold and warmth are present simultaneously. When they work together like this, many other beings will be present as well.

Sometimes when I go out to enjoy the sunny warmth of a cold morning, there are many other beings enjoying it with me. There are birds, flowers, even flies. I don't know where they come from. I just stand there observing the overall picture of my life, which includes the lives of other beings and the cold, bright, sunny morning. It's really a peaceful feeling. I can't say it's warm. On the other hand, can I say it's cold? Our consciousness always wants us to pick up one or the other. But if we do, pretty soon we will say it's too cold or there are too many flies. This is just to attach to our sense of self.

In order to understand our territory, we have to go beyond it. We have to go to the place where we can see the overall picture of human life. But we can only do this by throwing away our egoistic sense of things. As Dogen put it, depending on our commonsense view and egoistic notions while seeking the highest level of human life is like driving our cart northward when we wish to go south.

To seek the highest level of human life is very difficult. Most people are curious, but they don't want to practice. It seems too hard. Nevertheless, whether you can leave behind your physical and intellectual desires or not, move toward that level, little by little, day by day. This can be your effort.

The fact is, we are always just present in Totality. There is nothing to do but just stand up in the midst of cold, warmth, flies, pretty flowers, birds, clouds, sunshine. Being here is not theory but fact. To realize this fact is to have no sense of ego.

No confusion,
no question, no doubt

THE TEACHINGS OF BUDDHISM come from the Buddha's own experience—from his awareness, his wisdom, and his compassion. Their purpose is to help us in the realization of Truth. The Buddha's wisdom comes from our innate capacity to see what life truly is. This is not just a matter of human life; it includes the life of birds, plants, animals—of all beings. Every one of us has the ability to understand our life and the life of the world. Every one of us can attain wisdom.

In Buddhism, wisdom does not refer to our usual type of understanding—that is, understanding based on concepts. Wisdom is deep and direct understanding, which, unlike conceptual understanding, is without confusion, questions, or doubt.

In the *Nirvana Sutra* it says that if a cow drinks water, it becomes milk, but if a snake drinks water, it becomes poison. Still, we all drink the same thing. In other words, we all have the same ability to understand water. In terms of wisdom, we all live as equals in the vastness of the universe. But we manifest differences according to the attention our wisdom receives.

For example, sometimes Katagiri turns into a cow. He drinks water, which then turns into milk to help all sentient beings. But sometimes Katagiri turns into a snake. We become snakes when we possess the three poisons of greed, anger, and ignorance. When we're blind to Truth, when we don't understand ourselves, we're greedy and full of attachment. But if we learn to observe ourselves, we can be free from the three poisons.

Still, we all drink water. We all swim in the same ocean—the snake, the cow, everyone. We are all equal, but the quality of our swimming differs according to the degree to which we create poisons.

Our original nature is based on wisdom. Ultimately nothing can really obstruct our ability to understand human life. All we have to do is simply take care of our life—observe our life and see how we're actually living from moment to moment. This is to be free of the three poisons of greed, anger, and ignorance. As Dogen Zenji said, to learn Buddhism is to learn the self. And to learn the self is to learn the Buddha's wisdom.

Wisdom often appears in everyday life as compassion or kindness, such as when we see a baby and give way to a smile, even though we may have been angry just a moment before. This is our innate wisdom coming up naturally, according to circumstances. When wisdom works in our everyday life, we call this "living in vow"—living in our profound aspiration to help all sentient beings. *Vow, wisdom, learning the self*, and *our great ability to understand human life* are all different terms, but their meaning is the same. They allow us to manifest ourselves, surrounded by compassion, in the vastness of existence.

Learning the way of enlightenment

THE PURPOSE OF BUDDHIST PRACTICE is to learn the Way. Learning the Way is not like what we learn at a university or trade school. If we want to live the spiritual life, we have to study something more than what our consciousness allows us to see. We have to realize the world beyond our little life. This is no small matter. It's boundless. It's a huge matter that consumes your whole life.

The spiritual life is not about beliefs in mysterious or miraculous things. It's about learning something immense and profound, something greater than any idea you can have. This "something" is the Way; it is universal life. Even though you don't understand it, it is what we set out to attain. This is why we practice. This is why we live.

To learn the Way is why the Buddha was born into this world. It's why *you* were born into this world. The fact is, you are Buddha. Our practice is to see this great matter. We can't say this practice is either easy or hard. Nor can we treat it lightly. Whether we know it or not, it comes from the bottom of our life.

Eka Daishi (Hui-k'o), the second Zen patriarch in China, asked Bodhidharma to accept him as his student. When Bodhidharma rejected him, Eka Daishi cut off his own arm and stood outside in the snow to demonstrate to Bodhidharma the strength of his intention to study the Way. If we view it in our usual way, this example seems violent and cruel. But for Eka Daishi it was not cruel. Nor was it easy or hard. Beyond any ideas *we* may have about this situation, Eka Daishi realized there was a great matter he had to face.

Eka Daishi's desire for enlightenment came from the bottom of his life. No one forced him to cut off his arm. The act came naturally from the strength of his spirit. Beyond any ideas of hard practice or easy practice, all he had to do was devote himself to negotiating the Way.

In praising Eka Daishi's example, Dogen said, "Men of the present day say that we only need to practice what is easily practiced, but their words are very mistaken and far removed from the Way." It is only when we see everything from our usual, egoistic point of view that we use labels like "hard practice" or "easy practice." Furthermore, if we say we only need to do easy practice, soon someone will tell us we need to do hard practice. Then we will get in an argument or just be confused.

But why emphasize hard practice? Why emphasize easy practice? To insist on either means we still don't realize the true importance of what we seek. If we really touch what is important, then very naturally the Way-seeking spirit comes up. Then, whatever people say, you just do what needs to be done. People will criticize you; that's very natural. If a hundred people look at you, each one of them will try to give you a different idea. But as Dogen Zenji said, their words are very mistaken.

When we see the example of the second patriarch, we may say, "This is impossible for people in our modern age." Of course, we shouldn't cut off our limbs or go to some other extreme. But this doesn't mean we should ignore Eka Daishi's example. His desire for enlightenment was expressed in a way that was natural for him and that fit in with his culture. The point is that, beyond the labels of "hard" or "easy," he had to express his deep aspiration.

If we want to, we can make hard practice out of anything— even lying down. But our practice is to manifest perfect tranquillity within each form our everyday activity takes—getting up in the morning, having breakfast, going to work, walking down the street, and so on. So, it's our intention, not "hard practice," that's important. Beyond discussions of hard or easy, just practice the Way.

Purity of mind

THE ORIGINAL NATURE OF EXISTENCE is invisible and indescribable. It has no particular form. Whether we are conscious of it or not, we live in the original nature of existence.

On the other hand, in our subjective experience, we see this original nature as particular things: trees, clothing, food, flowers, birds, stars, and so on. It is through seeing, touching, and feeling that we can realize there is more to our experience than the forms we perceive. Through the tree we can see free, vast, open space extending in all directions.

When we see the form of the tree, we don't just see the form of the tree. But if we try to explain or describe what is more than the tree, we find it is indescribable. We can't touch it. It has no form, no color, no smell. Yet we realize something is there, something vast and open. We call it "truth."

But this truth is only the semblance of Truth. It is not real Truth, because real Truth has no form. That which has form always appears subjectively. If you really experience Truth, it's very difficult to say what it is. We can only explain original nature as it takes the form of a tree, of our food, of the stars.

Form and no-form always occur together. And though they are clear and obvious, we always get caught by them. If we *see* these two at once, however, it's called *seeing* Buddha, or *seeing* Reality.

To *see* Truth, we must be free of both form and no-form. In *seeing* Truth, no gap appears between subject and object. No gap appears between ourselves and others. In Buddhism this is called purity of mind.

But look at how our ego-consciousness works, and look at how stubborn we are. In the United States there are many races—African, European, Asian, Native American. When meeting a person of another race, it's easy to hold to a particular form and create a gap. I am Japanese; for me it's easy to feel a gap between myself and Americans. It's not so easy to practice purity of mind.

If we practice very hard, day after day, it's possible to experience purity. But then we attach to that purity, and suddenly the purity of our experience is no longer pure.

This is why we have to practice continuously. Practice must flow like a river—quietly, smoothly, continuously. If we would experience purity, we have to practice like this.

The first moment

ZEN MASTER NANSEN ALWAYS SAID he knew Truth, so a monk asked him, "What is it? Are you always there?"

Nansen said, "I don't know."

"I don't know" means "I'm not in the first moment." Being in the first moment is to see each aspect of everyday life as it is. This is egolessness. It's very simple. But if you say "I'm always in the first moment," that's attachment. That's why Nansen said, "I don't know."

The monk then said, "If you don't know, how do you know you are there?"

Nansen said, "You're pretty smart, so just bow and leave."

That's pretty good, isn't it? Our consciousness constantly asks, "How do you know?" That's a pretty smart question. We want to know, but how can we if we *don't* know?

The first moment is beyond any idea we might have about it. But if we simply see Reality as it actually is, then we can see where we are. So just put your body and mind right in the first moment. Then you will see the whole panoramic picture. It's just like being at the top of a high mountain.

We want to know things intellectually. We want to get a grip on things. So we think, we study, we do research, thinking we can trace things all the way back to their beginning. But in doing so, we lose the panoramic picture of Reality. We will never get the full picture through intellectual understanding. Rather than trying to know reality through the intellect, just put your body and mind at the top of the highest mountain. Practically speaking, this means to enter the first moment. In other words, just be *here*. Then you can *see*. Then you can wake up.

The first moment is both the creation of samsara—the world of suffering and delusion—and the realization of nirvana. In the first moment, we can take care of the samsaric world. But this is not our usual way. The first moment is very profound, refined, and undefiled. It means your deeds are appropriate to what is actually occurring here and now. In the first moment, you can act very simply, clearly, and straightforwardly. It's not a matter of coming to some decision by way of our calculating mind. It's not a matter of choice.

The first moment is pure and transparent. There we can see to the bottom of the samsaric world, where there is nothing to analyze and nothing to think about. There we can see what is Real; we can see the profound basis of human life.

Returning to this first moment is our practice. It is not something we can have some idea about. It's something we have to live. To be in the realm of the first moment, we have to work—simply, clearly, silently, and steadfastly. This is a little difficult, but we have to do it continually. How do we wake up to the first moment? We don't know. Do we awaken only after understanding how we awaken? No. We awaken before we understand, before we poke our heads into the first moment.

Returning to the first moment requires high resolve. This means we have to practice without excuses. We just do it. With high resolve our ego is purified. Selfhood drops away very naturally. In Japanese this is called *shikan*, or wholeheartedness. It is single-pointedness of mind. With such a mind, you respond perfectly to whatever situation you are in. It's like driving: you apply the brake before you think, "I don't want to hurt that squirrel!" You just do it.

It is only *after* the first moment that you see the world of conscious thought. This doesn't mean to ignore the conscious world, which arises in the second or third moment, the fragmented world of things and our attachments to them—that is, the samsaric world. But in Zen practice we are most concerned with what occurs at the *bottom* of the samsaric world. Our main concern is not the second or third moment but the first.

If you practice in the realm of the first moment, you will find wisdom and the functioning of wisdom. You will find beauty and the root of wholesomeness. Actually, though, you are never without any of these, because they are planted at the bottom of your life. But because our consciousness is, by necessity, always involved in the complications of the world, we don't accept this. Still, you can make your mind very clear and simple by going to the bottom of the multifaceted world of consciousness, and then you can see how the first moment works. Then, very naturally, you are free.

To accomplish this is difficult, I know. That's why the Buddha gave us skillful methods. In Mahayana Buddhism, we have what are called the six perfections: generosity, the precepts, effort, patience, wisdom, and meditation. By practicing these perfections, we come to the source of samsara. In going back to the source, there is a kind of astonishment. It's not something you can pin down, but it touches your heart. It's like meeting a moose on a country road. When you really face the moose, the whole world is a surprise.

Be in the first moment. Practice there. This is how Mahakashyapa attained enlightenment when he looked at the beautiful flower held by the Buddha. It's how Master Kyogen attained enlightenment when he heard the sound of a pebble hitting bamboo. His experience of hearing that sound was in the first moment—and it rang clear. Immediately Kyogen participated in the vastness of existence. Or consider Master Gensha, who attained enlightenment in the moment he stubbed his toe on a rock and cried, "Where does this pain come from?"

The first moment is nothing but astonishment. If you practice deeply on a daily basis, you can meet this astonishment for yourself.

No substantiality

IF YOU REALLY WANT TO KNOW what human life is, you have to see deeply into what in Buddhism is called nonsubstantiality. The Buddha's teaching of nonsubstantiality means that each thing is an aggregate of other things. In other words, there is no particular thing called "I" or "you" or "book." So, even though I say "I'm Katagiri," this is just a kind of fixed idea—a very narrow understanding. If I become attached to it, I feel that I am separate. But Katagiri can exist only in relationship with others. Without you, the floor, the table, or Minneapolis, Katagiri can't come into existence. The same, of course, goes for you.

When you look at your life, you judge yourself. Sometimes you put yourself down; sometimes you're proud of yourself. But whichever way you go, you don't hit the mark. Judging yourself in this way doesn't help you to understand yourself; it doesn't indicate how you can better live in human society. Every day, every moment, there is always the question: "How should I live with others?" To live only for yourself seems easy, but it doesn't work. It separates you from society and from the world. You have to put aside your own ideas about yourself. You have to see yourself from a universal perspective.

There are always those who fight with others. As we look around the human world, it seems we have no idea how to live in peace and harmony. We see so much fighting that we say we are unable to live together. As soon as we say this, however, it becomes our idea. And no idea can touch Reality. Instead, what we have to do is find a way to live in peace and harmony in a world that seems to offer us no idea of how to live in peace and harmony. This is our way.

If you think, "I have found a way to live in peace and harmony," that's fine. But if you get attached to it, it won't last. Sooner or later it will cause trouble. Peace and harmony are not just an idea. You have to find a way to actually practice them from day to day.

The teaching of nonsubstantiality refers to the unity of all things. We have to taste the truth of this deeply in our bodies and minds. No matter who you are, Buddhist or Christian, as a human being you must find a way to live in this world. For this the experience of realization is necessary. Tasting realization deeply is the first point of Dogen Zenji's teaching. The Buddha called this right view, or right understanding.

The second point of Dogen's teaching is practice. Practice means acting with wholeheartedness. But generally, before we can be wholehearted about anything, we want to know things—we want some intellectual understanding as background. This type of understanding is important, of course, but it can't take care of the whole of our lives.

Life is vast. There are lots of things about our lives that we simply can't understand. Still, at minimum we need some information on how to act. If you listen to the Buddha's teaching, you may not understand it all, but maybe some of it sticks in the corner of your heart. Perhaps just a sentence, or even a word or two, impresses you deeply. You don't understand, but you're moved by it, and then someday, later on, while you're reading a book, perhaps, or quietly listening to the teaching, suddenly you understand it.

We must work this understanding—that is, we must refine it, deepen it, and live in accord with it. In other words, we need to practice. Practice means that we mindfully participate in life as the flow of time itself.

For example, when you are in an airplane, you can see time as an object. But when you do, time, the airplane, and you are all separate. This can create a lot of fear. I often travel by plane, and in my heart there is always a little fear, because my consciousness always sees time and the airplane as separate from me. This is not right understanding.

Where am I? In the flow of time. The airplane, the clouds,

the sky, the whole universe, and I are one Reality. My death and my life are One. So I should be mindful of the total situation of my life—which includes the airplane, time, life, and death. With this awareness, I become a little more quiet. If I can see the whole situation as One, I can taste impermanence and no substantiality deep in my body and mind.

Still the ego can get in the way. Thinking "I became a little more quiet" is not good enough. It's still egoistic. But can I think, "I *am* quiet"? No. This still is not perfect. How about "I am"? No. "I"? No. Only when the "I" is one with the total situation is there true quiet.

When you drive on the freeway, perhaps it seems that you experience yourself, your car, and time as separate things. But you can taste them as One. As you try to taste this unity, however, they will still be a bit separate. You can't escape from this separation just through your thinking; you must taste the unity with your whole body. When you do this, you will have no ideas about being separate from your car. You are just there, driving. This is to manifest your life in simplicity. This refined human action is practice.

To understand your life, you have to see it in its unity with other beings. This universal life is the Buddha Way. Dogen Zenji said that in the Buddha Way, all things exist in realization.

But there is something else for us to do. We must practice total reality—that is, we must practice oneness beyond realization. To be free from all attachment means you must live even beyond realization. To be free from what you have tasted very deeply means you can actually put it into practice. This is to participate—organically, directly, simultaneously—in the flow of nonsubstantiality. Regardless of whether we fully understand it or not, our way is to practice this teaching through and through, day by day, with our whole body and mind.

The top of the head
of zazen

Kᴇɴᴅᴏ, ᴛʜᴇ ᴡᴀʏ ᴏғ ᴛʜᴇ sᴡᴏʀᴅ, is one of Japan's martial arts. It is something like the sport of fencing, but with a bamboo sword. The object in a kendo match is to hit a precise spot on the top of your opponent's head. If you hit the exact spot, you get a point. But if your sword slips, even just a little bit, you get no point.

We might say the same of zazen. If you are sitting in zazen, you have to hit the head of zazen just so. Most people get lost in daydreams or sleep, and they hit the side of zazen. But if you really want to do zazen, you have to hit it right on the top of the head.

We call our practice of sitting in meditation *shikantaza*. *Taza* means "precise sitting." To sit precisely is to hit zazen. To hit the head of zazen is *shikan*. *Shikan* actually means "nothing but" or "wholeheartedness." It is one-pointedness of mind. To sit this way is to manifest your life in simplicity, beyond your speculations of good or bad, right or wrong.

In kendo, if you hit the side of your opponent's head, you should realize your mistake. You should then be aware of where the top of the head is. Then, with your whole body and mind, just aim for it. Constantly aim for the top of the head.

Like so, you should ask yourself where the top of the head of zazen is. Aim for it with your whole body and mind. Try to touch the top of the head of zazen with your consciousness. If you do just this, someday you will hit the top. Even though now you can only hit the side of zazen's head, don't be disappointed.

You must participate in the practice of no reward. In other words, don't cherish your understanding. When you think "This is good zazen," you should be free from such thought.

Even though you think "This is bad zazen," you must be free from this as well.

Be mindful of the top of the head of zazen, and constantly aim at it. And then, one day you will hit it. How does it happen? I don't know. But someday, somewhere, you will hit the top of the head of zazen. You will be surprised. It is beyond your comprehension. But suddenly, after much practice, there is success.

So don't be discouraged. Don't be proud. Be free from it all. Just look to where the top of zazen's head is. Continue to practice.

When you can't move an inch

WE ARE SELFISH. We can't get away from it. At the same time, we can't say with conviction, "I must live with my selfishness." In other words, we can neither escape nor stay with our selfishness. Still, this doesn't mean we should think we can't be free of selfishness. The question we must ask is, How can we take care of our selfishness?

When we are driven into a corner and we can't move an inch—this is precisely where the Buddha Way helps us. When we are in this difficult place—which is where we spend our lives—we have to do something. This is what the Buddha's teaching is all about. But it is not about getting an *idea* of how to get out of this corner. This teaching is about letting us know just what our situation actually is. In the case of selfishness, it is about letting us know what selfishness is, how it works, and how we can best deal with it. *This* is our practice. This is why, in Buddhism, we study the human mind in great detail.

Our purpose is not to get some *idea* of how consciousness

functions. The ideas we come up with—whatever they are—are always limited. When we hit the limits of an idea, we want to dump it and move on to some other idea. If it begins to dawn on us how dismal this process is, we can get pretty depressed. This is where practice comes in. Practice allows us to go beyond such limitations. So we have to understand deeply just what practice is.

If we are to take care of it in the best way, we have to open our hearts completely to our selfishness. This means that if you see others as your enemy, you have to realize that *you* are the enemy, not them. You have to realize that as you look at them, so they look at you. You have to let them look at you until you become the object instead of the subject. You have to look at yourself until you see yourself as they do.

Usually we look at everything just from our own perspective. We just look at "them," and that's it. But in doing so, they are always separate from us, and we are cut off from them. With this understanding, we can't accept others at all.

When we see things only through our intellect, all relationships appear frozen. This makes all relationships into ideas. Very naturally, then, you and I appear as separate beings.

The relationship between you and me is not something static. It's in motion constantly. When we look deeply, we see that both subject and object are nothing but constant motion as well.

The Buddha's teaching is about accepting both subject and object as they appear together in dynamic movement. It's not merely an idea. It's Reality, and we can *see* it directly.

Going beyond

THE FIRST LINE OF THE *Heart Sutra* tells of Avalokiteshvara, the bodhisattva of compassion, practicing *prajna paramita*, the perfection of wisdom. The sutra's last line is the mantra *Gate, gate, paragate, parasamgate! bodhi! svaha!* which roughly means, "Gone, gone, gone beyond, gone altogether beyond!"

To practice this perfection of wisdom is to taste Emptiness. We can't really practice Emptiness, because it is too subtle. It is empty even of itself. But we can practice perfect wisdom. Actually we are never apart from perfect wisdom, from a very deep understanding of human life. Still we have to deepen our understanding constantly, until it reaches "Gone, gone, gone beyond, gone altogether beyond!" This going beyond is not just for you personally. To go beyond your conventional understanding of things, all sentient beings have to go beyond with you. This is Avalokiteshvara's practice.

To move deeply in the perfection of wisdom is to feel compassion for others, to be one with others. For example, if you deeply understand trees, very naturally you will have deep compassion for them, and you will act in accordance with this compassion and understanding. As you experience compassion for trees, you will become one with them. Your life will then become like art or poetry.

But still you have to deepen your understanding, day after day. Only then can you truly love and merge with other beings. Then you will naturally share your life with others, and others will share their lives with you. It's like learning the tea ceremony. In the beginning you must always follow the rules. But if you continue to practice, you will soon not pay any attention to the rules. Even though you are not aware of it, your capacity to perform the tea ceremony will have matured. Beyond the rules and regulations, the actions of the tea ceremony will manifest themselves very naturally. Your movements will become perfectly consummated, beautiful beyond words. But you will not know why, and you will have nothing to explain.

If you practice Zen like this, you will begin to see how beautiful your life is. You will move like a summer wind. Your actions will be free and flexible. Like dancer and audience coming together, something electric—like sparks flying—happens between you and others. This is spiritual communion, the true meaning of Emptiness.

Medicine and disease

BUDDHISM TEACHES THAT the ultimate nature of being has several remarkable features. The first is that it is vast, all-pervading, and seamless. The second is that it lacks form, color, smell, and flavor.

The third feature of the ultimate nature of being is that it acts at super speed, yet it is always tranquil and very quiet, which is the fourth feature. In being quiet and tranquil, it reveals the active aspects of human life. This is why, if you sit down in zazen, you can begin to see the highly active aspects of your body and mind.

The working of the third and fourth features is coincident. Because of this, if your life is too active, you are not satisfied. On the other hand, if you are always quiet, you don't like that either. Activity and tranquillity must work together. In everyday life, you have to find tranquillity in activity and activity in tranquillity. This requires great resolve of will and a clear mind.

The fifth feature is that, because nature is very active, things are constantly arising and perishing. All things are interconnected and arise together, yet each thing arises under different conditions. You appear under different circumstances than Katagiri does; trees arise differently from birds. But we all arise together in this moment—active, yet very quiet. Sometimes we fight, sometimes our lives are bustling, but at the bottom of existence all is tranquil and serene. Like a calm lake or the quiet figure of a tree on a peaceful morning, all life is very quiet yet active. Everything works together, smoothly and freely. This is the actual life of a tree, a bird, a pebble. It is your true life.

The sixth feature is that when we are conscious of something—say, a tree—precisely and clearly as it appears, all beings appear along with it as the very quality of its life. Seeing a tree is like picking up a single frame of a net—the rest of the net follows. Though the other frames of the net appear behind, they are not separate from the frame you have picked up. When you look at your life, you have just picked up the single frame of a net. If you look again, you will see all beings following, becoming the contents of your life. Unfortunately, this is not our usual way. We are very egotistical. We work against the basic rhythm and nature of existence.

Even though all beings exist in this moment, the single frame your consciousness picks up appears to be absolutely alone. If you pick out yourself, you will appear to be alone, too. This is the seventh feature of the ultimate nature of being. Of course, in Reality you *are* alone, but not in the usual sense. To be perfectly alone is to be One with all beings. It means that all beings support you. In other words, you are really alone not as your small self but as all beings. But the moment "you" appear, the rest of all beings appear—not in front of you, but giving their support from behind. As Dogen said, "When you see one side, the other side is obscure." When one side of your life, the subjective side, appears large and clear, then all other beings—trees, birds, and other people—appear behind, supporting you.

Zen master Ummon once said to his community: "Medicine and disease subdue each other." In other words, when you pick up disease, the whole world becomes disease. But in the next moment, if you pick up medicine, the whole world be-comes medicine. Still, strictly speaking, the basic nature of existence cannot be pinned down to anything particular. Is the whole world really disease? No. Is it medicine? No. Only when you pick up a frame of the net as medicine does the whole world become medicine.

In a commentary about this case, Zen master Yuan Wu quotes a story from the *Avatamsaka Sutra:*

> One day Manjushri ordered Sudhana to pick medicinal herbs. He said, "If there is something that is not medi-cine, bring it to me." Sudhana searched all over, but there was nothing that was not medicine. So he went back and told Manjushri, "There is nothing that is not medicine." Manjushri said, "Gather something that is medicine." Sudhana then picked up a blade of grass and handed it to Manjushri. Manjushri held it up and showed it to the assembly, saying, "This medicine can kill people and it can also bring people to life."

Sudhana was seeking Truth. He had already visited fifty-three teachers before he came to see Manjushri. But after this discussion he attained enlightenment—so this is an interest-ing discussion.

In using the word *medicine*, we are speaking of the dualistic world. There is sickness, and it stands in opposition to medi-cine. Furthermore, sickness is thought to be bad, while medi-cine is thought to be good.

Consciously or unconsciously, we understand delusion and enlightenment in this same dualistic sense. But the Buddha said, "I, the great Earth, and all beings simultaneously attain enlightenment." This means that there is no gap between bud-dhas and ordinary people. But in the world of delusion, where we commonly live, having this dualistic sense is very natural for us. So if we compare ourselves to buddhas, we see our-selves as very ordinary and we see them as very wise.

Even though the Buddha said that we are buddhas, we don't believe it. We don't see the Buddha in our everyday life. It's as if the Buddha is hidden somewhere. That's why we approach practice as if we're trying to dig down deep into our lives and dredge up the Buddha. But this is very dualistic. If you continue to practice like this, it will be pretty hard to know peace.

If we practice zazen as medicine, believing we are sick, it is very difficult for us to realize the true meaning of practice. We always compare this with that, and then we ask which is good and which is bad. But there is no peace in it. There is no security, assurance, or relaxation. This is why we find it difficult to be peaceful and harmonious from day to day.

If we contemplate the Buddha's statement "I, the great Earth, and all beings simultaneously attain enlightenment," it will become the form and content of zazen. Sudhana couldn't find anything that was not medicine because everything goes beyond its own frame. Beyond our likes or dislikes, each form is the complete actualization of Reality. In Reality all things work together. There is no difference between them; they all participate freely of the Whole. This is why grasses, tables, birds, clothes, all things—even a piece of toilet paper—must be taken care of with kindness, consideration, and a charitable heart.

The front and back of life

DOGEN ZENJI SAID, "The great path of the buddhas, in its consummation, is passage to freedom, is actualization."

Whatever object you are focusing on, there is always some aspect of it—whether it's a book, a chair, the floor, the light, or the air that surrounds you—that goes beyond its own framework. This is actualization. But what is truly actualized is not anything you can see with your senses. It can't be apprehended through our notions of right and wrong, good and bad, like and dislike. What is truly actualized is beyond the dualistic world.

With actualization, we don't see life as opposed to death. Life is something more than any idea we can have about it. When life is completely actualized, it functions with death. Like life, death is greater than any idea we can conjure up in our minds. It is more than just the opposite of life. When we try to deal with death as though it were something opposed to life, it scares us. But death is the complete actualization of Reality. It is based in freedom. Life passes out of life to freedom; death passes out of death to freedom. This book, the floor, the light—all things empty themselves and pass through to freedom in the same manner. This is complete, perfect actualization.

Just before he was about to die, the Zen monk and poet Ryokan was asked, "What do you think about life?" He responded with a haiku: "Maple leaf, falling down, showing front and back." Life is just like a maple leaf falling. "Falling" means that your life is marching toward death, marching to the graveyard. And on the way to the grave, what happens? Your back shows. Your front shows. You show grief, you show pleasure, you show suffering. That's it. This is life.

Someone asked me to write Ryokan's words in calligraphy, but when I did, I added one more thing. I wrote, "When the maple leaf falls, there's no failure in its fall." Do you understand? Right in the midst of falling, there is no failure. "No failure" is completely beyond success and failure. This "completely beyond" is not abstract. "Completely beyond" refers to what is truly actualized, which is complete and perfect, beyond our petty thoughts of good and bad, beyond our likes and dislikes.

The falling of leaves is why the scenery in autumn is very beautiful. Sometimes when we feel the impermanence of life, it makes us pensive or sad. But it's just autumn. Even in the fall of a single leaf, we can realize how the whole world becomes autumn. A single leaf shows autumn exactly as it is. This is not abstract. This is our life.

Living a bodhisattva's life

MAHAYANA BUDDHISM CENTERS on the idea of the bodhisattva. *Bodhi* means "Enlightenment," and *sattva* means "being." Originally, the term *bodhisattva* referred only to Siddhartha Gautama before he became the Buddha, the awakened one. But by the first century of the Christian era, the term *bodhisattva* came to apply to anyone who has the aspiration to awaken.

Traditionally, the bodhisattva is a person who seeks Truth, or Enlightenment. But *bodhi* is not separate from *sattva*. *Bodhi* is *sattva*. Therefore, we are all already bodhisattvas, enlightenment beings.

The bodhisattva's life is based on wisdom and compassion. Wisdom is seeing deeply into life. This means that we do not assume that we are alive only by our own effort, but we see that we live by the efforts of all other beings. Bodhisattvas put the comfort of others before their own. To think of others before yourself is to live a bodhisattva's life.

As bodhisattvas, we want to understand the human world. So we have to study wisdom and compassion. This doesn't involve a lot of mystical stuff; it's just a matter of observing human life very deeply. In doing this, there are a few practices we should consider. One is throwing away arrogance. Arrogance is the firm belief that "my life is mine." Whether we are psychologists, secretaries, or scientists, most of us carry on with this belief. But this is very dangerous because it is to act out of the belief that we can actually control human life by our own will. If we can see the arrogance in this belief, we can learn to be humble. To practice humility is to cultivate wisdom. By throwing away arrogance and practicing humility, we express our universal life.

To be considerate of others, you must also be considerate of yourself. You must take responsibility for your own life. Only in this way can you truly see the lives of others and consider them before yourself. Consideration of others extends beyond just other human beings to include all things—tables, cushions, even toilet paper. We must be considerate of all things and treat them with great appreciation and respect.

This is not a matter of discussion. It is a matter of practice. First the flower opens, then its petals fall, then comes the fruit. The flower is the Buddha's teaching, and the petals are the daily events of our lives. When these things are received as the life of the universe, we can appreciate them as we would the Buddha's life. If we learn to treat each thing as Buddha's life, our arrogance is easily thrown away. When we handle things in a warm spirit and with a kind heart, the Buddha's life will manifest in our own lives.

To live as all beings

IN THE *Vimalakirti Sutra*, to bring out his great wisdom, Manjushri, the bodhisattva of wisdom, asked the layman Vimalakirti how bodhisattvas should regard all living beings. Vimalakirti answered that they should see all beings as provisional and transient—as flashes of lightning, as bubbles on water, as drops of dew, or as air waving in the heat. Then Manjushri asked how bodhisattvas should deal with these provisional and transient beings. To this, Vimalakirti said that all beings should be treated with compassion.

Buddhism is not a matter of discussing metaphysical questions, like whether we should deal with our lives as real or unreal. Buddhism is about accepting life totally and handling it with compassion. This compassion is open to everyone.

In Buddhism, compassion is that great and generous warmth of heart that goes beyond commonsense notions of kindness. It cannot be understood by means of explanation. In fact, life itself is not something we can understand through explanantion. The movement of life is completely beyond our dualistic thoughts of good and bad, right and wrong. This means that right now, right here, we have to take care of life, as something provisional.

The state of being provisional is the Truth of our lives. Again this is not something we can understand intellectually. Having some idea of provisional being is not what Vimalakirti meant. When Vimalakirti spoke of "provisional being," he was referring to Reality, to the True nature of your life. Your life is not something particular or definite. Even so, if you don't take care of this provisional being prudently, you will create problems. This is why, under all circumstances, you should take care of life with compassion. Just put yourself in the middle of life— interconnected and interpenetrated with all beings—then act. This is a very practical way to live.

To live this way doesn't mean you must know the details of everyone's life or have a lot of intellectual knowledge. As Dogen Zenji said, "A bird's life is not an idea; it is to fly the sky." If we only understand the bird intellectually, in terms, say, of biology, we can talk about it endlessly. But no matter how long we explain the bird in this way, we never really touch the bird's life. The bird's life is to fly.

Does the bird understand what the sky is? I don't think so. But flying is what it does, what it has to do. Flying is the bird's urgent need of the moment. When you want to drive your car, you don't wait until you understand all the workings of the engine. You just turn the key and drive.

Turning the ignition key seems to be a small act—just a tiny seed. Yet it is not a tiny seed, because when you turn the key, all kinds of energy—remote and immediate—come together. In the moment you turn that key, the countless efforts of people, many different materials, even time itself, are realized. This tiny seed is the whole universe.

Turning the key is not merely turning the key. You have to open your eyes to see not only the key but all the beings behind the key. When you deal with the key like this, the key becomes life itself. Practice this way and you will understand what it means to deal with all beings with compassion.

Participating in the life of the world

LIKE PHYSICS AND BIOLOGY, Buddhism is an attempt to study things as they are. But in Buddhism, particularly in Zen, what we study is something more than what appears as objects to our minds. You might wonder how we can look at something that is not an object. But even though something doesn't appear as an object, it nevertheless manifests itself in the realm of practice.

Through zazen we can understand things as they truly are, before we conceptualize about them. But if you want to do zazen, you have to learn true zazen, which is something more than the zazen that runs through your consciousness. To do zazen correctly is to immediately go beyond all distinctions. This is difficult to understand, but it is what we are actually trying to learn.

We usually handle zazen with our conceptualizing mind and our emotions. What we think we want to learn is the zazen that will satisfy our desires. But as long as we continue to poke our heads into it, human desire is never satisfied. When we read or think about zazen, it is far from us. It is something we want to get some idea about. By sticking with our ideas, we slip away from zazen and we slip away from life as it truly is. So we have to learn to realize what we know directly, before we fall into thought.

Dogen Zenji, in *Tenzo kyokun*, (*Instructions for the Cook*), instructed cooks not to view food in the ordinary way. He said a cook should be able to build a palace from simple grains. In other words, we should express the Dharma even through the most trivial activities. Because such objects are not separate from us, in dealing with a cabbage leaf, a pan, or a slice of bread, we have to do the Buddha's work. If we handle such things as mere objects, if our handling of them is based only on how we think or feel about them, we will deal with them carelessly. Whatever you feel, just deal with each thing directly, as it is, beyond your likes or dislikes.

We already have ideas about nature, so it's pretty hard for us to deal with nature as it truly is. Still, we want to learn about nature. And we want to know what the difference is between nature and ourselves. But this is where we slip. We create the idea of nature, and thus we create lots of trouble as well.

Nature is dynamic, always moving, changing constantly. But the movements of nature are not reckless. Beyond our ideas and concepts, there is a principle at work behind the movement. There is total functioning, the working of the Whole. If you want to learn zazen, you have to learn this principle of being. We call this principle Dharma. Unlike the arbitrary rules we might prescribe for ourselves as religious doctrines, this principle is the principle of existence itself. Whether we know it or not, everyone must comply with it. But Dharma is not something we can hold as an object in our minds. We have to participate in it.

It's winter now, and the tree outside the window obeys the reality of winter. Like so, you must also deal with winter as it is. You can't deal with it according to just your feelings and emotions. Beyond your likes and dislikes, you have to obey winter as it is. Then winter will penetrate your life, and you will learn what winter really is.

Existence is nothing but motion and change. Motion and change penetrate the entire universe. They are the life of trees, the life of winter. They are your life, too. So if you examine your life, you will find the whole universe therein. Your life manifests as the activity of the Whole. The total activity of the Whole manifests as you.

Still, whatever we say about Dharma doesn't hit the mark. So the question we must ask is this: using this body and mind, how can we participate in the life of the world after throwing everything away?

The host within the host

THE EIGHTY-FIRST CASE OF *The Blue Cliff Record*, "Shooting the Elk of Elks," reads:

> A monk asked Yao Shan, "On a level field, in the shallow grass, the elk and deer form a herd: how can one shoot the elk of elks?" Shan said, "Look—an arrow!" The monk let himself fall down. Shan said, "Attendant, drag the dead fellow out." The monk then ran out. Shan said, "This fellow playing with a mud ball—what end will there be to it?"
>
> Hsueh Tou commented, saying, "Though he lived for three steps, after five steps he had to die."

How can you shoot Truth as it is? That is, how can you be master of yourself in any situation? If you understand this, you can shoot the elk of elks.

Dogen Zenji said that although you may practice samadhi

(concentration) in zazen, you really must find the king of all samadhis. You can't be caught or bogged down with conceptual awareness. Within conceptual awareness, you must be free of conceptual awareness.

We can find various kinds of concentration—in sports, in art, in everyday life. In whatever people do, we can find many kinds of samadhi. For instance, in wintertime you put on winter boots and clothes before you go out, yet you're not aware that you have put on winter clothes. You have become one with your winter clothes; you have melted into your object. This is samadhi.

If you notice your experience of samadhi, you might start to enjoy it too much. Then you will stumble over it. But the important thing is not to keep your samadhi. What is important is to be free of it. This will only happen if you learn not to cling to a particular object. If you don't cling to a particular object, you will become free of the subject—you will become free of yourself. This is becoming one with your object.

The Song of Jewel Mirror Awareness ends with these lines:

> Practice secretly, working within
> As though a fool, like an idiot—
> If you can achieve continuity,
> This is called the host within the host.

This has the same meaning as shooting the elk of elks.

If you become a host within the host, you appear just like a fool or an idiot, because your practice is not very showy. If your practice is climbing a mountain, you must become one with the mountain. As you climb, your life is very quiet and unsophisticated. Under all circumstances—through dangerous situations and complicated procedures—you continue to climb, unafraid and undaunted. Such a life is quiet, calm, and very unusual. You go unnoticed by others. If someone happens to notice you, you appear only as a fool, an idiot.

But if you get tied up in a particular task, you become

merely a host for the guest. This is our usual way. You become bound up and exhausted. To experience being a host for the host, you forget yourself and become one with your task.

Because we don't see into the depths of our lives, we generally don't understand how important this is. Our lives run deep, but we are always swimming on the surface. So make your mind calm and clear, and sharpen your eyes. Then you can see into the depths of your life. This is to become a host within the host.

The introductory comment to "Shooting the Elk of Elks" reads:

> He captures the banner and seizes the drums—the thousand sages cannot search him out. He cuts off confusing obscurities—ten thousand devices cannot get to him. This is not the wondrous functioning of spiritual powers, nor is it the suchness of the basic essence. But tell me, what does he rely on to attain such marvels?

"He captures the banner and seizes the drums" refers to someone who has become one with his object. Before you is the mountain, and you have to climb it. As long as you see the mountain as your object, you feel you have to conquer it. Because of this, many things, both physical and mental, come up—fear, pleasure, pain, joy, uneasiness. But beyond all this, you have to deal with the mountain. In other words, in order to climb it, you have to embrace the mountain right now, right here.

"The thousand sages cannot search him out." How can you become one with the mountain? How can the flame of your life melt into the rock? Intellectually, it's impossible. But if you really become a mountain climber with a sincere heart, you can experience this. It really depends on you. The task you've set out for yourself is not the problem. The problem is always in yourself. If you become free of your task, then you can really take care of it. But if you are not free of it, if your ego is always coming up, then the task becomes a burden.

Our usual way is to deal with each situation through our ego. If we don't like what we're doing, we quit. It might seem that handling things this way will give you pleasure, but it's not really the best way to take care of your life. Even though you don't like it, you have no choice. You can't quit. Just climb the mountain. Though the situation may be dangerous, there's no way to escape. Beyond your likes and dislikes, just make yourself one with the mountain. Though you go through many complicated procedures in climbing the mountain, your life goes on in a very simple way, because there's no choice.

"Ten thousand devices cannot get to him." Simplicity in our lives always helps cut off confusion. But where does such power come from? Whatever kind of information you collect from whatever source, you will never find an answer to this question. All you have to do is be free of ego.

"This is not the wondrous functioning of spiritual powers." This isn't something mysterious. If someone asks, "If I practice hard, will the universe take care of me?" how can I say yes or no? It is not within our power to determine what the universe will give us. Furthermore, to expect to be given something wonderful is not true freedom.

"Nor is it the suchness of the basic essence." In other words, this power doesn't come from Buddha or Dharma or God or anything you can name. It isn't limited by your conceptual thought.

What is the ultimate source of existence? Just to speak of it means you are already separate from it. The ultimate source of existence has nothing to do with either duality or oneness. If you say one word, you are already bathing in the dualistic world. But this doesn't mean you shouldn't bathe in the dualistic world. In fact, you *have* to bathe in the dualistic world. But if you take a bath after working hard, or after being outside in the cold winter, what is there to say when you step into the nice warm bath? All you can say is, "*Ahhh!*"

Within this simple expression of your life, this "Ahhh," there is no particular object called "bath" and no particular subject called "you." The water and your body have become one. This is the functioning of the source of existence. But the moment you speak of it, your body is immediately separated from the source of existence. Analysis of where this "Ahhh" comes from is just the work of your conceptual mind.

We already live in the realm of freedom. Still, we have to take care of the conceptual, dualistic world. The question is, how can we experience freedom within our conceptual awareness?

Because we have the power of intellection, this is a big problem for us humans. Birds, pebbles, trees—all sentient beings live on the same ground we do. But because human beings have the ability to conceptualize, we live in a world of duality. Although we dichotomize the world into subject and object, the world is not actually dualistic. Strictly speaking, we humans, like all other sentient beings, live in nonduality. But we must realize this nonduality through duality.

"But tell me," the commentary continues, "what does he rely on to attain such marvels?" How can the mountain climber become one with the mountain? Or as it says in the main case, "How can one shoot the elk of elks?" How can one shoot the essence of peace and harmony and experience them from moment to moment?

In the main case, Shan says, "Look—an arrow!" In other words, "Look! It's already been shot. There's no chance of missing; there's nothing to explain. Your peaceful, harmonious life is already here. Look!"

The monk then fell down, pretending to die. In doing this he was saying, "If the arrow has already pierced me, I'm dead." But when Shan said, "Attendant, drag the dead fellow out," the monk jumped up and ran out. In other words, if you want to be one with the object and freely express yourself, you have to die. That is, you must become egoless. To die to the ego is not to be dead.

No. It is to live with the mountain, the snow, and the blue sky. When the monk ran out, he demonstrated life within death.

But Shan said, "This fellow playing with a mud ball—what end will there be to it?" The mud ball is thought, conceptual awareness. In testing his teacher, the monk discriminated too much. His efforts just resulted in the creation of a lot of thought.

Hsueh Tou offers the comment, "Though he lived for three steps, after five steps he had to die." In other words, being a host for the guest—playing with the objects of your mind—can only go on for so long. Even if you carry it on for a hundred steps, eventually you will have to die.

Just look at your life. You go to school, you study hard, and you get graded by your teachers, who really admire you because you are a good student. But now grades are what you are running on. How far can you go? Fifty steps? A hundred steps? Maybe even a thousand steps? But this kind of living usually doesn't last very long. Our circumstances are always changing. And we change. Everything is changing, and we don't know what will happen next.

Even though we do well in school and get good grades, we eventually run into disappointment. Then we ask ourselves, "What will I get from more school? Will that make me feel good?" If you become interested in Zen, you will then ask, "What will I get from zazen?" But where is the peaceful life you are always looking for? Where is the spiritual life you say you want to live? What are you looking for anyway? We don't know it, but what we are always looking for is a way to become a host for the host.

Vimalakirti was a greatly awakened layman who lived in a small room only six feet square. A story in the *Vimalakirti*

Sutra tells of a time when he was sick in bed and five hundred monks and bodhisattvas went to him to pay their respects. When they got there, one of the Buddha's disciples, Shariputra, doubted they could all fit in Vimalakirti's room. There weren't any chairs for them, and there wasn't much space. So Shariputra asked Vimalakirti how they could all get into his room. Vimalakirti said, "Did you come here seeking a chair or seeking Dharma?" Dharma, of course, is Truth, and the chair stands for our concerns for the mundane world. Shariputra answered, "I am here to seek Dharma." Suddenly all five hundred monks and bodhisattvas entered Vimalakirti's small room.

Of course, to the intellect this story is impossible. How can five hundred monks and bodhisattvas get into such a small room? We don't have any idea. Yet they do it. How many cells and nerves are there in your body? Yet the moment you do something, the moment you think or move your hand, millions of cells and nerves—not merely five hundred—work together, simultaneously and in harmony.

Or consider the mountain. How many beings exist there? How many worlds exist together in the same space? There are worlds of insects, of rocks, of plants, of birds, of people. How do they all come to live together as one in peace and harmony? We don't know; yet they do. You can become one with the thousands and millions of beings—birds, trees, rocks, pebbles, air, dust particles—that all live together in the small room called the mountain. But this happens only when you are a host for the host, when you are where everything comes up together.

If you are always seeking the spiritual life according to your commonsense understanding of things, you can go on for a while—five years, six years, maybe longer—but it won't work. You know that sooner or later you will have to die, so your practice brings no peace or harmony. This is why Hsueh Tou made the comment, "Though he lived for three steps, after five steps he had to die."

There are two ways to take care of your life. You can develop yourself as an artist, or you can forget yourself and devote your life to art. That's a big difference. The first is to enslave yourself in your ego. It feels good for a while, but it doesn't last for long. This is to become a host for the guest. The second way is to become a host for the host. You must turn your ego into fuel and burn your life for the benefit of all beings. You will become a kind of fool. But this is the way to find peace. Just climb the mountain, every day.

Becoming a good hunter

IN HIS COMMENTARY ON THE KOAN "Shooting the Elk of Elks," Zen master Hsueh Tou tells us:

> The elk of elks—
> You should take a look.
> (Yao Shan) releases one arrow—
> (The monk) runs three steps.
> If he had lived for five steps,
> He would have formed a herd and chased a tiger.
> The correct eye has always been given to a hunter.
> In a loud voice Hsueh Tou said, "Look—an arrow!"

The phrase "Look—an arrow!" indicates that Truth is not something far removed from you. It's right under your feet. The arrow has already struck. It has already done its work. This arrow is active and dynamic. No one can stop it. It strikes the moment it acts, so there's no time to discuss how, what, or where.

Master Ryokan's poem about falling maple leaves showing their back and front speaks of two states of existence. One is "showing back and front"—in other words, material form. The other is "falling."

As we perceive forms through our senses, we put labels on them: "good," "bad," "woman," "man," "doubt," "trees," "rocks." All things—mental and physical—appear as form. But what makes this appearance possible? Behind the forms we experience, there's something else that we pay little attention to. That is falling, or activity. Without activity there is no creation of form. There is no showing of front and back. And without form, activity is not defined or understandable.

But we're always focused on just the phenomenal world of form, of front and back. We don't pay any attention to what's behind phenomena. It is very difficult to grasp, so we just concern ourselves with what we can grasp easily. We are just interested in the skin. But behind the surface, behind the forms, there is something active and dynamic. This is what Ryokan was speaking of.

Activity produces the phenomenal world of form. Though the world of phenomena shows both front and back, we usually involve ourselves with only the front. We have to see the front when the front is showing, but we must also see the back when the back is showing. And behind whatever shows, we have to see the activity and dynamism that no one can grasp. When we try to hold on to the front, it turns into the back; when we try to hold on to the back, it turns into the front. There is nothing we can hold on to. Still, we have to take care of this world of phenomena.

This is a little difficult for us adults. A baby's consciousness, on the other hand, is like a ball floating in the middle of a stream. For a baby, objects appear and then they are gone and forgotten. For adults, when objects appear, we stay with them and play with them. This is what gives us the sense that things persist. But behind any object there is nothing but activity. We sometimes call this activity the life force, we sometimes call it Truth. It is really the universe, the Whole. It is not a concept. You can't hold it in your mind as an object. Nevertheless, the arrow has already found its target.

Within activity we see "front" in three steps and "back" in five. Life and death. But three steps is in five steps. In other words, right in the middle of life, you have to die. Right in the middle of death, you have to act. You have to be alive even while death embraces you. Thus the monk ran out. Right in the middle of death, he's alive.

Now you are alive. But simultaneously you die in each moment, because there is nothing to hold on to. To really do something means that you die. True life as it is, infused with death, is total freedom.

If you take care of your life—knowing that it is both life and death and that it is backed by activity—you will see that your life is surrounded and supported by many beings. This is why, had the monk lived for five steps, he would have formed a herd. This herd is all the beings of the world—not just human beings, but all beings, both animate and inanimate. If you take care of your life properly, as life and death, it will naturally involve all beings. Then once your life includes all beings, you can live with them in peace and harmony.

We usually believe that our problems are "out there": in society, in nature, in other people. But our problem is with us. It's ego. Consciously or unconsciously, we attempt to take care of our life by satisfying our ego's desires. We even sit zazen to satisfy our egoistic desires. But sooner or later we must ask ourselves why we're sitting zazen. Is it really to save all sentient beings? It is a beautiful idea, but I don't think that is why most people do it. Most of us sit to save ourselves. This is why we have difficulty taking care of the sangha. We are just concerned for ourselves. For most people, it is the self that comes first.

Behind your form there is something always acting. It pervades everything and everyone. If we attach to what only appears on the surface of things—if we don't pay any attention to the activity beneath the show of front and back—then we don't see that the universe is all within ourselves. Then we try to keep away from the enemy we think is "out there."

Hsueh Tou said, "The correct eye has always been given to a hunter." To truly practice zazen is to allow yourself to be free of you. But if you tie yourself up with the idea of you yourself sitting zazen, then you are not truly practicing. You are just a particular person sitting there. You are not expressing what is universal. True zazen is when you are free both from yourself and from your object. If you don't understand this, you will always be concerned about your object, and you will never be a good hunter.

To be a good hunter means being free of your object. If you are free of your object, then, naturally, you are free from the subject—you. If you do zazen perfectly, there is no you practicing zazen. You become free from the practicer. To be free of the practicer of zazen is to be free of zazen as an object. It is to truly be here.

And so, in a loud voice, Hsueh Tou said, "Look—an arrow!"

Finite and infinite mind

SINGLE-MINDED DEVOTION can be very unwholesome if it doesn't take into account the world as a whole. Usually we say, "I want to do this, but I don't want to do that." We always make choices, emphasizing ourselves first. But if you become infatuated with something, you become crazy. If I say, "Do zazen with wholeheartedness," you might become crazy about Buddhism and zazen.

To do zazen with true wholehearted devotion is not to be infatuated. It is to practice with mindfulness and concentration; it is to arrange a noisy mind into a calm mind. But even when we try to practice like this, questions still come up. This is because we've forgotten the world as a whole. The more we try to make our minds calm in this forgetful way, the more noisy they become.

Just collect the mind. Bring your mind to the quiet, one-pointed devotion of simply sitting. This is taking care of sitting, taking care of breathing, taking care of your mind, taking care of the world as a whole. It's not thinking; it's not excitement. There is no concern for the degree to which you collect your noisy mind into a mind of peace and harmony. If you are measuring zazen, then you are practicing not with wholeheartedness but with infatuation. If you say, "I sit zazen wholeheartedly," this is not wholeheartedness either. Wholeheartedness is doing something without any need to measure or to look around. It is not about whether you feel good or bad, nor does it have to do with discussing how well you are focused. If you approach zazen in this way, questions will bubble up in your mind, and off you will go chasing about for answers. You will be creating a fractured world of this and that, because you are practicing in exchange for what you can get. You are doing zazen with yourself in mind.

In Zen we speak of the Mind that is transmitted from generation to generation. This Mind is all sentient beings. It is infinite Mind. Because Mind is infinite, there is nothing to get. It is always with you. Wherever you may go, this Mind is you. But the moment you speak of "my mind," you remove yourself from it.

Since wherever you go there is universal, infinite Mind, then be open. Give yourself up. This is not about discussing psychology or analyzing your personal feelings. It is completely beyond any of that. A Zen master said to a monk, "You must see the universe in your cup." The monk looked into his cup, but he didn't see the universe there, so he threw the cup away. The Zen master said, "Oh, poor cup." We think the cup is too small to hold the universe. Intellectually, we can't see how it could fit. But wherever we go, the whole universe always appears—in a cup, in a window, in a smile, in a word. We have to learn to see this.

PART THREE

You Have to Say Something

The source of existence

THE MONK TENNO ASKED his teacher, Sekito Kisen, "What is the meaning of the Buddha's teaching?"

Sekito said, "It is unattainable and unknowable."

"Will you say more?" Tenno asked.

The teacher said, "The great sky doesn't bother the function of the white cloud."

Truth—the source of existence—is unattainable, unknowable. But if I say "unknowable" or "unattainable," you might then believe you cannot attain, touch, or Know Truth.

If you think the source of existence is over there and you are here, this is a dualistic understanding. The source of existence is not a thing. Although you are never apart from it, if you say, "I am one with the source of existence," you will feel a gap. In Reality, however, there is no gap. The source of existence needs no explanation. But it doesn't matter whether you explain it or not. It supports your life and the life of all sentient beings. The source of existence is the source of existence.

Because you exist, you see the world from your point of view. Because many things connect with your individual life, you cannot ignore your individuality. This is why Buddhism teaches Dharma—Truth—with explanations that are connected with your individual life. That is why Buddhists have developed extensive systems of philosophy and psychology. But Dharma remains unknowable and unattainable. No concept can hold it. Because of this, it is free.

Whatever you see in your life and in the world is the source of existence. And it is all unattainable and unknowable. This means that your life and the world are completely beyond thoughts and ideas. This is a little difficult to understand because human consciousness always separates and dichotomizes, dividing the world into subject and object. Although the source of existence is beyond the function of your consciousness, although you cannot attain it, nevertheless it works with you constantly. Strictly speaking, it is every aspect of your mind and each pore of your body.

As an individual, you see all existence as occurring in time. When the source of existence manifests in time, it appears different in each moment. At one point you see a book, in the next moment a cup, in the next moment a hand. But basically, book, cup, and hand are all the same—the source of existence.

It takes time to understand the Buddhadharma. How long should it take? I don't know. But don't be hasty. You want to understand by way of your discriminating consciousness. You want to know, want to know, want to know. Finally your knowledge is broken into pieces. You don't know what's going on. There's just total confusion.

So don't be rushed, particularly when it comes to understanding the Dharma, the total picture of human life. You try to know the total picture of human life, but your knowledge is very small. How can the huge universe fit into your small world? It's impossible. Instead, why don't you fit your small world into the huge universe?

Beyond what your senses reveal, your life is intimately connected with all sentient beings. From moment to moment, you live at the source of existence. So don't be hasty. Make each step stable. Because whatever you do occurs within Truth, within Dharma, you should walk as best you can. You have to take care of this moment with stability and majesty.

I don't mean you shouldn't try to understand. But no matter what you understand, through concepts the source of existence remains unattainable and unknowable. Ultimately you don't know what human life is. This doesn't mean that you should give up. You cannot be lazy in trying to understand. You have to understand—but you cannot hurry. When each step of your life is stable, very naturally, even before you're conscious of it, the source of existence will penetrate you, like the wetness that soaks your dress when you walk in the mist.

Human life appears and disappears like the tiny flowers that bloom in the heart of the mountains. If you see such a tiny flower, your heart says, "Oh, poor, tiny flower, why don't you bloom in the beautiful garden? People will pay attention to you there."

But this is just noisy human desire. The tiny flower doesn't care about being noticed. In reality, the tiny flower exists as it is, at the source of existence, blooming in the heart of the mountains.

Buddhadharma is unattainable, unknowable, yet is this something you cannot Know? No. Buddhadharma works every day. The great sky doesn't bother the function of the white cloud.

Life beyond explanations

MOST OF US WHO LISTEN to the Buddha's teachings probably have some reason for why we started listening. Those who do zazen probably have a reason for going to the meditation hall. Some will say it's to have a happy life. Others might say they want to make their life free of all the complications in the world around them. Some just simply want to make their body and mind healthy. But whatever the reason, it is not what is essential. Explanations are just secondary.

I don't mean that we should ignore our reasons, because they might be very important to us. But we will never truly digest our practice by offering explanations about why we do it. The essence of the spiritual life is that it goes on without limits. In other words, your life is not limited by your life. Thus it gives us great hope. But hearing this, you might start to think that there is something in you that exists eternally, even after you die. You might say, "The soul exists forever." If you believe this, you are what is called an eternalist. On the other hand, if you don't accept eternalism, believing that there is no soul, then you are a nihilist. These are the two basic views of life. But whichever one you pick—eternalism or nihilism—it doesn't hit the mark.

If you look at your life with a calm mind, you can see that your life holds the past and the future right now. Your life is not just the thin piece of paper we call the present. It is actually very thick, very profound. There is depth to your life that runs beyond all your ideas and speculations. To live a spiritual life is to reach to the depths of human life, which run beyond our intellectual understanding and beyond our present life. Why did you start reading this book? Why are you interested in Buddhism? Why do you want to practice meditation? You may offer reasons, but finally you don't know why.

I came to the United States in 1963. I have been here for many years. But if I look over my life, I can see that there are many things I haven't done. For instance, it is said that Buddhist literature contains eighteen thousand scriptures. I became a monk at eighteen, but still there are lots of scriptures I have yet to read. As much as I would like to read them, my life is not long enough to do all the things I want to do. No matter how long we live, how can we satisfy all our desires? If you try to finish all the things you want to accomplish in life, you will become very nervous, irritated, and uneasy.

Human life goes on forever—life after life. But as soon as I say this, you think, "Katagiri believes in reincarnation." But the human life that goes on life after life is not your life, or my life, or anyone's life in particular. If we attach to eternalism, thinking that there's some particular identity that persists life after life, we will suffocate right in the middle of the dark dream of eternalism. When this notion ceases to satisfy us, we will look around for something that does. We will struggle to find some explanation that will satisfy us, eventually falling into nihilism, but the same dissatisfaction occurs. No matter which way we go, there is always uneasiness and dissatisfaction.

Actually, reincarnation occurs moment after moment. But we should never attach to it. "Attach" means to see in it a persisting entity. This is very important to understand. We must not create an "ism."

If you attach to the explanation of eternalism, your life will no longer be rooted in the earth. Your heart should just accept all sentient beings as they are—as nothing in particular, as completely fluid. The spiritual life requires us to practice tasting this truth. To do so is to experience a generous, magnanimous mind.

The total picture of life and death

LIFE AND DEATH ARE NOT TWO. Life and death constitute a single event. We usually don't see life and death in this way. Instead we imagine there is some space between them, like the space we imagine between ourselves and other things. This is ignorance.

Ignorance means we don't realize what is Genuine and True. We ignore that there is really no gap between ourselves and others. But we imagine that there is. This gap is intellectual space, philosophical space, psychological space, cultural space, emotional space, time space, spatial space, and on and on. Our minds create many kinds of gaps, and then, in accord with this, we put names on what we think, see, or feel. But Dharma shows no gap between you and what you see or think or feel. Regarding life and death, then, there is really nothing apart from ourselves that we can put a name on.

Buddhism teaches that ignorance and Dharma work together as one. But when we see Dharma—which is clear and pure—we always put a name on it and turn it into ignorance. This is delusion, and because of our delusion, we don't understand things correctly. We have lots of misunderstandings. This would not be such a problem if we did not believe our understanding is really correct. We attach to our understanding and apply it to our work, our experiences, our memories, and so forth. But the total picture of the world is more than our deluded thoughts and misunderstandings.

Life and death are based in illusion. You cannot lay your hands on them. They apply neither to you nor to what you think, see, or feel. They are like waving images in the heat. The total picture of life and death is like a single sheet of paper. One side is imaginary; the other side is pure. If you touch one side, immediately the other side appears, while the side you touched disappears. But the moment you say, "Oh, it disappeared!" that side immediately appears again. These two sides, working together as a single event, are the total picture of life and death. This is not something we can comprehend with our ideas. The total picture of life and death works beyond human speculation.

Death and inseparability

WE DON'T KNOW HOW to deal with birth and death. We don't know how to deal with a person who is going to die. We don't know how to deal with our own mortality. Yet we must all face the reality of impermanence.

There are three points to look at here. The first is that we have to understand human suffering deeply. Suffering and pain are always with us. Even if you attain enlightenment— even if you become a buddha, a bodhisattva, or a saint—pain and suffering never leave you. The more deeply you see, the more you feel even the minute vibrations of suffering coming up from the depths of your heart. Our deep suffering becomes especially conspicuous in our last moment.

People have a preconception that when you become a Zen priest you have to die peacefully, preferably in a sitting position. But I don't think there is any particular pattern to how you should die. You may have ideas about how to die or about what a happy death is, but when you are actually faced with death, there are no guarantees about what will happen. When you face death, there is no space to look at death as an object. You are right there. Even in the face of death, you have to understand how to live from moment to moment.

Those who are about to die experience many complicated emotions—feelings of despair, sentimentality, and anger. This is very natural. But finally, they reach a stage where they completely give up. They realize that there is no solution and there is nothing to grasp. Within the realm of resignation, their consciousness still vibrates minutely with deep human suffering.

While facing his own death, a Zen master was asked about it by his students. He said, "I don't want to die." The students didn't expect such an answer. They believed that their teacher was a great Zen master. They thought a Zen master should say, "I'm happy to die." But, in fact, he was present with his suffering, with his no-solution.

The second point is that, in dealing with a person who is about to die, you can have a feeling of togetherness. When you think about death, you feel a separation between yourself and the person who is dying. But this is just an idea. In Reality there is no separation. You and the dying person are one.

A man who was soon going to die wanted to see Zen master Ikkyu. He asked Ikkyu, "Am I going to die?" Instead of giving the usual words of comfort, Ikkyu said, "Your end is near. I am going to die, too. Others are going to die." Ikkyu was saying that we can all share this suffering. Persons who are about to die can share their suffering with us, and we can share our suffering with those who are about to die.

Ikkyu's statement comes from a deep understanding of human suffering. In facing your last moment, you can really share your life and your death. If you are with someone who is about to die, you can massage her back, hold her hand, serve her a drink of water, or just sit with her. If your heart is warm and compassionate, even though you don't say anything, your presence naturally affects her.

This kind of feeling can't be developed overnight. You have to practice it from day to day. This is why I always talk about everyday life, which is made up of innumerable small things. Even though you don't like it, you have to take care of them— and other people—with compassion.

The third point I want to make is that we are constantly in the realm of Oneness. The Buddhist understanding of the world is different from our usual understanding. Our ordinary idea of knowledge is that it comes from drawing distinctions. We separate and classify all the various things of the world, and then we analyze them, again and again. Then we synthesize these various entities, looking for ways to bring them together. Only *then* do we look for Oneness.

In Buddhism, our approach is much different. Our understanding is that *before* we discriminate and separate everything—trees, pebbles, mountains, rivers, oceans, sentient beings, and all other things, both visible and invisible—all are One. Originally, before we poke our heads into the world and divide it into separate entities, all are One.

According to our usual understanding, to say that all are one is to say that all beings are one within a realm of separateness. In terms of Buddhist understanding, however, Oneness is the fact that each being is already within the realm of Oneness as the Whole.

If Oneness is truly Oneness, then you are exactly you. But then, who are you? What can you say? You have no idea. Yet Reality is completely clear and obvious. The trees, the sky, and all sentient beings know exactly who they are because they are already within the vast realm of universal existence. All you have to do is just be there—not as you, but as the Whole of Reality.

The Buddhist way of understanding the world makes it clear that it is not necessary to have a conceptual understanding about life and death. One person struggles and screams in the last moment; another prays to God. One person chants the name of Buddha; another expresses anger and hatred. That's fine. Whatever way a person dies is fine. The point is, however we view death, when we face it we must be present right there in the middle of the vast universe, which is completely beyond our speculations of good or bad, right or wrong. Our life is nothing but an endless stream, a dynamic flow of energy. All we have to do is just be there in the last moment. But the last moment is very quick. When you are in the last moment exactly, you don't know it.

In his essay "Zenki," Dogen Zenji said that life is the total manifestation of life, and death is the total manifestation of death. In other words, the momentum of life-and-death is beyond our ideas. So when the time comes for you to face death, all you have to do is return to the very first moment. In the first moment, we can realize Dharma. Dharma—Oneness, Totality, Wholeness—needs you, whoever you are.

LIFE IS THE UNIVERSE. It is the huge expanse of space and time. It needs no explanation. But if I don't say anything, you won't understand.

You exist at the intersection of time and space. This is your place. Although there are countless other such intersections, all these countless intersections come together in such a way that we can't separate out any single location. So a location is not really a location. Each location already completely occupies the vast expanse of time and space. This is the universe as One. This is where we live.

So, what should we do? That is, how are we best to live our lives? Well, we can't just sit down. We have to do something, because there are two aspects to the universe that are always present. One is stillness; the other is dynamic working. They are one Truth.

Dogen said we must penetrate *this moment*, again and again, forever. This is the most important thing we can do. There is nothing to change, nothing to hold on to, nothing to get caught by. All we have to do is constantly approach *this very moment* with a true heart. But this is not so easy.

How, for example, can we deal with a person who is certain to die soon and is now suffering terrible, unimaginable pain? Whenever we try to deal with such a problem by using some idea or rule, or by using our emotions, we create problems. All we can do is go into *this moment* with full awareness and do our best to deal with it as it is.

A man traveling in India came upon some people sitting around a cow that was about to die. He looked at the cow, and then he looked at the people and said, "Please don't just sit there looking at the cow's suffering. Shoot her as soon as possible. I don't want to see her suffer." But the people said to him, "No. Just sit here with us and watch."

This seems pretty odd, but it is a very direct teaching. We can't eliminate suffering; it goes on. We don't understand intellectually what death is, or what life is, because our thoughts can't get a grip on them. If we try to touch life, it is not really life, and if we try to touch death, it is not death. If in desperation we grab for mercy killing, it is not real death that we grasp but only our fears and ideas of death.

We have to take care of death as it is. Real death can only be faced directly. To do this we have to come into this moment. Death is not an idea. This is why real death makes us suffer, particularly when it is at a little distance. Seeing someone die scares us, because it is not really another's death. It is our death.

In the United States we try to take care of people who are dying by giving them a lot of attention. Then, when we send the dead body to the mortuary for preparation and to be put in a casket, we believe this is death. But this is not death. Death is never apart from life. So even while the person is still alive, we have to see death. Even now it is within us. We are all marching toward death.

We are in the universe—the Whole—regardless of whether we are aware of it or not. All we have to do is just live there. How? Without attaching to life or death, just being present in each moment. We can't attach to either because they are both always present at once. If you can stand up in *this moment* with a true heart, immediately you will experience true affirmation of yourself as the Whole. But in the next moment, you have to let that experience go.

Letting it go is returning, once again, to *this moment* as it is. Then the next moment appears just as it is, and you can face it, naturally, with freshness of mind. But if you don't return to *this moment*, the real moment will not appear. You will just be caught up in your idea of the moment. You will never totally participate in it; you will never accept *this moment* as completely new. You will be stuck in your thoughts, your memories, and your preferences, which bubble up from your mind and cause you to waver.

As simply as you can, you have to just stand up in *this moment*, and then let it go. Then you can be in this moment, and you can be in the next. It's just like breathing in and out. If you exhale completely, you inhale in the next moment. And when you finish inhaling, exhaling comes next. This occurs naturally, even before you're conscious of it. Inhalation and exhalation work together as one. So stand up in *this moment* and experience it totally; then just let it go. Let each new moment come up fresh, just as it is. To do this constantly is our practice.

Before thoughts arise

THE PRACTICE OF ZEN BUDDHISM is understanding life as the constant flow of activity rather than as concepts and beliefs. This is particularly true of Dogen Zenji's teaching. But when I say the world is more than our concepts, immediately you are confused. There is nothing for you to get hold of. Consciously or unconsciously, you try to depend on a conceptualized world.

The Buddha and other great teachers have always pointed to the world that is here *before* we conceptualize it. We have to taste this world and understand it as it is. Conceptualization is important, of course. It is a kind of blueprint of the world that we draw upon. We can't live without a blueprint. But neither can we live inside a blueprint. We become onlookers in the world of concepts. We look and think and imagine, and though we study our blueprints, we don't understand just what it is that we are imagining.

When you burn paper, you probably think that the paper is something other than the fire. This is the world of conceptualization. But actually, there is no separation. Paper is fire. Fire is paper. But even saying "paper is fire, fire is paper" is dualistic.

If I talk of my death, I can't explain the reality of it in words. Why? Because first I have to say the subject, I. Next comes the verb, die. First there's me, who isn't death, and then comes "dies." It's very dualistic. In Reality, things are not separate in the way they are in language. The paper is fire. I am life, I am death. There is no gap between them. But we get used to understanding the world through the concepts we use to describe it. This is why, no matter how long we discuss this problem, we don't get it. We have to *just see* it.

Zen master Gasan was asked by his master, Keizan Zenji, "Do you know there are two moons?" Gasan didn't understand, but he contemplated this statement for three years. Gasan's practice was very serious and very deep, and eventually he understood Master Keizan's point.

If we see the moon in the sky, we would say it is just one moon. But this is just our common understanding, the understanding of our conceptual mind. It is not really *seeing*. When we conceptualize, we always bring ourselves up first. When we say, "I see the moon," there is some separation, some duality. But in Reality, you and the moon are merged completely. Our practice is to see this Reality in which there is no separation between "you" and "moon."

Beyond our likes and dislikes, something is constantly happening. Beyond all human criticism and evaluation, life goes on. In Reality, your life is always being supported by many things. This is why Master Keizan told Gasan that there are two moons. There is the moon we conceptualize and there is the moon as it is, completely interfused with all beings. If I see the moon, I am moon.

Conceptually, we believe there is one moon. And of course it is so. But the moon of our thought is not the real moon, because the conceptualizing mind always inserts the self first, before we acknowledge the moon as it is. But beyond mundane thoughts and speculations, you and the moon are wondrously interfused. This is True Reality. It is not an idea. It is inconceivable. It is where you and moon are interidentical. This is our life.

The flow of the moment

FOR MANY PEOPLE LIFE IS like a vending machine. We put coins in at the top, push a button, and get results from the bottom. We don't care about what goes on in between. We think it's not our business—it's the machine's business. This is modern civilization. So when it comes to practice, we think all we have to do is put the coin in. We receive zazen instruction, and we expect that in the next moment a Pepsi-Cola will roll out. We completely forget the moment-to-moment process of practice.

At first we sit with the expectation that something wonderful is going to happen. But as we continue to sit, we learn how we participate in the flow of time. Gradually we begin to pay attention. Gradually we begin to notice a shortening of the distance between cause and effect. Gradually we learn to see that at the very moment we touch the coin, the result appears—a Pepsi-Cola!

In eating a meal, what is the shortest time between cause and effect? If we become one with eating the meal, we don't know. All we have to do is eat. Each day we wake up, but it is only in the instant *after* we have awakened that we realize it. Within waking up, we have no idea of waking up. Our practice is to be in the flow of this moment, before we put a label on it called "waking up." Because we are already one with waking up, this is waking up as it is.

When we are in the flow of the moment, cause and effect,

subject and object, all appear together. You can't put a label on this moment. Yet this moment is working. It's alive.

Zen texts have many stories about awakening to this basic nature of existence. In one such story, the sixth patriarch asked one of his students, "Can you grasp vast, open space?"

"Yes, I can," answered the student, and he reached up, grabbing at empty space.

"That's good," said the patriarch, "but it isn't grasping space as it is."

The student said, "How do you grasp space as it is?"

Immediately, the patriarch pinched the student's nose. The student screamed, "Ouch! Too rough!" But within his very own scream, between the time he said "Ouch!" and "Too rough!" he attained enlightenment.

The point of studying Buddhism is not to put a lot of stuff in your head. It is to guide your consciousness closer and closer to the original nature of existence. This is "space-as-it-is." How do we awaken to this? Just participate in the flow of *this moment* as it is. Just open your heart.

Cutting off the flow
of time

IN THE SEVENTY-FIRST CASE OF *The Blue Cliff Record*, "Wu Feng's Shut Up, Teacher," Pai Chang asked Wu Feng:

> "With your throat, mouth, and lips shut, how will you speak?"
> Feng said, "Teacher, you, too, should shut up."
> Chang said, "Where there's no one, I shade my eyes with my hand and gaze out toward you."

Even though we don't know what we're looking for, we all seek some explanation of life. We're constantly looking for something beyond the reach of our consciousness. We want to get at something that will verify our existence. This is the first stage of human suffering.

This suffering eventually makes us reflect on ourselves and our actions. Because everything our consciousness picks up is unstable, flighty, and changeable, it's difficult for us to feel relief from what appears. Even when we're happy, we still feel an uneasiness deep within our minds.

We try to approach Truth in many ways—through art, music, poetry, philosophy, science, religion, and so forth. We ask about the truth behind the sculpture, the painting, the poem. But what we can express in words is not exactly Truth. This is why we look to what's behind the poem. Behind the poem there is something that lets us feel relief. Still, we don't know what it is.

The spiritual life is about approaching Truth directly, without relying on any special techniques, instruments, or objects. By using only our bodies and minds, can we seek Truth directly? This is the problem Pai Chang was pointing to when he asked, "With throat, mouth, and lips shut, how will you speak?" Then, when Feng answered, Teacher, because you are asking us how we can speak of Truth with our mouths, eyes, and ears closed, you, too, should shut up, Pai Chang said, "Where there's no one, I shade my eyes with my hand and gaze out toward you." He said this because Wu Feng had cut off the flow of time between himself and Pai Chang.

We always discuss things in time. But if you touch Truth, you cut off the flow of time. You are then really present. But we don't recognize this. Instead we discuss things in the hope that we will come to some resolution. But the discussions never end, and ultimately they give us no relief. They don't answer anything. They only create more confusion. Still, we can't stop discussing things. Without words it is very difficult to know Truth. Even though we don't know how to communicate Truth, we still have to speak.

Imagine that you are driving in the country and suddenly you see a moose. You shout, "Wow! A moose!" Suddenly the whole world has become moose. The flow of time is cut off. But what is this moose? It's not something strange, really. We know what it is. We've picked up lots of ideas about moose. But when we actually see a moose, we're surprised. It is truly a moose beyond any discussion about a moose. You, the moose, and the whole world exist together right now, in the present—right in the middle of time, yet completely cut off from the process of time. Everything becomes the present. In the whole world, there is only one thing going on, and you have become one with it. The moose has become completely absorbed into your life.

You say, "Wow!" and though it is just a simple expression, it is very pure. You have given it no thought. This is clarity—clarity of existence, clarity of time, clarity of space. You can't explain it. You can only say "Wow." You meet this clarity of time and space that cannot be expressed, and then you can express it. Because no one is there, you can write a poem about the moose as it really is. The poem originates from a time and place where no one exists.

If you *see* this moment and this place, security, assurance, and repose appear. But even though I teach, explain, and express this spiritual security, you are still far from it. So, where there is no one, I shade my eyes with my hand and gaze out toward you.

Living in the universal marketplace

USUALLY WE BELIEVE we can know things through our senses. We believe everything is "out there."

We often act as if we understand everything, and we have a strong desire to show the superiority of our understanding. That's why we try to conquer everything—nature, other countries, other people—even ourselves.

This is, of course, a completely perverted view. It is very egoistic. When we see the world only in terms of ourselves, we lack a broad perspective. We cannot accept others—including trees, birds, rocks, and nature—as they are.

We think that all is as we see it. We are unaware of our ignorance. We are always rushing to a destination. We want to have an idea we can hold on to. We want to know. This is fine, but we should maintain a generous, tolerant heart and mind; otherwise we will become very egoistic, cerebral, and cold. This will make a lot of trouble for us. The growth of human knowledge seems to be good, because it has enabled us to create a better life for ourselves. On the other hand, we have created lots of problems: we have destroyed nature, we have destroyed people, we have destroyed many things.

When Baso said that he sat zazen to become a buddha, his teacher, Nangaku, asked him how he could make himself into a buddha by sitting. This question completely confused Baso, so he asked, "What shall I do?" Nangaku didn't answer him directly but gave only a hint. He said, "If a cart doesn't move, would you whip the cart or the ox?"

Commenting on this story, Dogen Zenji said, "Although it is not the custom among worldly people, the Buddha Way has the custom of whipping the cart." Of course, according to our usual understanding, if you want the cart to move, you whip the ox. This is the kind of logical thinking by which we manage and arrange the things of our world. In other words, whipping the ox represents the world that we can conceptualize. On the other hand, whipping the cart is the world we cannot conceptualize. Even though we forget that world, many things go on there.

The Real world consists of both a conceptual world and a nonconceptual world. But we ignore the world we cannot get in our hands. We just whip the ox. For instance, if your practice of zazen doesn't move, to whip the ox means you are trying to understand zazen intellectually. When you cannot understand it, you reject it. But Dogen says that according to the Buddha Way, we whip the cart. In other words, we can't hold zazen as just an idea.

Reality is not just the reality you understand. It is the Buddha Way, and even before you create any ideas or concepts about it, it is already present. This Reality consists of the merging of what can be thought of and what cannot be thought of. Words cannot touch it; there is nothing we can say about it. This place, where nothing can be pinned down, is where we actually live moment to moment. We can call this the universal marketplace. All sentient beings live there. This is why it doesn't work to try to take care of your life just according to your individual views. Instead, we have to settle ourselves in the whole, the universal marketplace. To do this is to hit the cart.

How are we to live in this way? Let me give a simple example. We use forks, spoons, and knives when we eat. The appropriate place for forks, spoons, and knives is the kitchen. If we stored forks in the bathroom, it wouldn't make sense. We don't use the fork as if it existed by itself, apart from the knife and spoon. But a fork should not imitate a spoon. A fork should just be a fork, but in the kitchen. In this way, the fork's life will naturally connect with the spoon's life even though, from moment to moment, the fork appears to be separate from the spoon and from the knife.

We always want to compare the fork with the spoon. In other words, we always see our life in comparison with others. We try to communicate with others, but how well can we communicate when our own life doesn't run smoothly? If you want to have communication, you have to operate just as you are. You have to operate as the very life of the universe itself.

If you think you can understand your life with just your ideas, you are ignoring where and how you actually exist. You are living your life just like a fork in a bathroom. It may seem all right for a while, but ultimately it doesn't work. You become completely isolated.

All things—good and bad, right and wrong—are manifestations of the Real world. But to attach to one thing or the other is to create suffering, isolation, and egoism. Attempting to purify your life through egoistic understanding can never bring true wisdom, because you will be unable to accept the great teaching that the world offers us.

There is a story of two men who survived being persecuted by the Nazis. One day, as they were walking together, they came to a barley field. The first man could see that there were young shoots of barley coming up, so he avoided walking through the field. The second man, however, said, "No, let's cut through the field."

Both of these men had survived the same horrid experience under the Nazis. But where one had become sensitive to killing, the other was filled with anger. For the first man, his tragic experiences taught him a great deal about how to live with all sentient beings. Horrible as it was, he accepted his past experience. His tragic experiences had taught him to open his heart to others—even to the barley shoots. This is great teaching the world offers us.

You cannot understand the world just in terms of your own views. You must accept the world as a whole—that is, you must be open to what you don't understand as well as what you do understand. In this way, you will become generous and magnanimous, and you will be able to receive what the universe has to teach.

A snowflake in a red-hot furnace

THE SIXTY-NINTH CASE OF *The Blue Cliff Record,* "Nan Ch'uan's Circle," states:

> Nan Ch'uan, Kuei Tsung, and Ma Ku went together to pay respects to National Teacher Chung. When they got halfway there, Nan Ch'uan drew a circle on the ground and said, "If you can speak, then let's go on." Kuei Tsung sat down inside the circle; Ma Ku bowed. Nan Ch'uan said, "Then let's not go on."
> Kuei Tsung said, "What's going on in your mind?"

Historically, in Zen teaching, a circle signifies Truth. So, in drawing a circle, Nan Ch'uan was asking Kuei Tsung and Ma Ku to say something about Truth. But that is pretty difficult, because the moment you say something it is no longer Truth. On the other hand, if you don't say anything, you can't help others to understand. So you have to say something.

There is no way to communicate Truth. So how can we express it, whether through language or some other way? And how are we to live in accordance with it? Like most cases in *The Blue Cliff Record,* this one contains a short introduction called a pointer. Here the pointer gives us a hint about how to bring our life into accordance with Truth.

The pointer begins, "There is no place to bite into." This is the total picture of Truth, the total picture of the universe. Truth is perfectly clear, tranquil, and serene. It is, however, completely without form. It has no flavor, no color, no smell. There is nothing we can say about it. We may have *idea*s about Truth, but Truth itself has absolutely no attributes. There is no place to bite into. There is nothing to touch.

Still, Truth is powerful and virtuous. It assists and supports all sentient beings. It is intimately close. We live right in its midst. When Truth functions within us, it is stable, strong, and beyond speculation. Because it is beyond our ideas, this functioning is called faith.

How does the working of truth manifest in individual life? Addressing this, the pointer continues, "Having passed through the forest of thorns, a patch-robed monk is like a snowflake in a red-hot furnace." The "forest of thorns" refers to the samsaric world—the world of birth and death, the mundane world of everyday events. It is the world as we usually think of it, filled with trouble, suffering, and pain. In this world of everyday life, we constantly create the three poisons of the mind: greed, hatred, and ignorance. To pass through the forest of thorns means to be free of these three poisons. The person who experiences such freedom is like a snowflake in a red-hot furnace. Each action the person performs melts away in the next moment.

If you throw a pebble into a very calm lake, you will create a ring of water. But the ring doesn't stay still. It expands and eventually melts away into the lake. It becomes the energy of the lake as a whole. This is similar to the way Truth manifests in our life. But this is not our usual way. Usually we are fascinated by the samsaric world. We refuse to let our emotions and experiences melt away. We put our snowflake in the freezer, and then we keep checking to see how it is doing.

It is difficult for us to become a snowflake in a red-hot furnace. But to do this is very important. We *must* do this because, even though Truth has no place to bite into, we cannot ignore it. Even though our bodies and minds exist in the samsaric world, we actually live in Truth. Even though we might not believe we can do it, our practice is to manifest Truth as best we can. This is the religious life.

The pointer then goes on to say, "Without falling into entangling ties, how will you act?" If we try to explain Truth completely, we will become entangled in our words. So the question of how then to act is most urgent. When Nan Ch'uan drew a circle on the ground and said, "If you can speak, then let's go on," Kuei Tsung immediately sat down inside the circle. In sitting down, Kuei Tsung was returning to his original nature. In this gesture he was signifying completion. You do the same when you sit in zazen. To do zazen is to return to the original nature of things as they are.

It is very difficult to see a tree through our senses just as it is. Our tendency is to see a tree according to our *idea* of a tree. But prior to our ideas, the tree itself exists as it is, as Wholeness. The same applies to our experience of what we call our self. Obviously we understand our self through all our senses. But in particular, we understand it through our *idea* of self. Consequently, our view of self is perverted.

But we cannot do this with Truth, because Truth is not an idea. We must see truth as it is. If we see Truth according to some idea, then it is not Truth. The tree standing in the yard. That's it! The falling snow. That's it! The tree is exactly the tree. The snow is exactly the snow. And sitting zazen is exactly sitting zazen. In sitting down inside the circle, Kuei Tsung was manifesting Truth.

Before we discuss what Truth is, or what the real nature of the self is, or what zazen is, or what kind of relationship exists between the real nature of the self and doing zazen, all we have to do is be one with the circle. All discussion and thought is secondary. It occurs only *after* the true moment has melted away.

To return to our original nature and to sit in peace and harmony, all we must do is be one with zazen.

After Kuei Tsung sat down, Ma Ku bowed. In doing so, Ma

Ku was expressing his deep appreciation and respect for Truth. He was demonstrating that there was nothing to discuss and no place for doubt to enter. Thus Ma Ku manifested Truth with a bow.

But then Nan Ch'uan said, "Then let's not go on." The meaning of this is not easily understood, so Kuei Tsung said, "What's going on in your mind?" In other words, "What's the matter with you?"

This is a very interesting conclusion. Though Truth is One, many beings exist. They retain their own forms, their own functions, and they manifest their own peculiar natures uniquely. "Peculiar nature" means that Katagiri is Katagiri. Katagiri is not mixed up with you, even though in Truth you and I exist as One.

All sentient beings are intimately connected. In Truth all things interpenetrate each other. Yet things don't become mixed up. Katagiri is still Katagiri; you are still you. This is very clear. All beings are interconnected, and this arrangement functions very peacefully and harmoniously. How? We have no idea, but we can *see* it is True.

If I see Katagiri merely as a conceptual form, it's not good enough. I must see Katagiri as interconnected with you and with all beings, because all beings exist as one. Yet, simultaneously, I have to see how you and I and all beings exist independently. Sitting down inside the circle was Kuei Tsung's way of expressing Truth. Bowing was Ma Ku's way of speaking Truth. They are different expressions, but they live as one in Truth.

But if we and all beings are already right in the middle of Truth, why should we have to seek it? *That's* why Nan Ch'uan said, "Let's not go on." Since it is not necessary to seek Truth externally, it was not necessary to visit National Teacher Chung.

Earlier, Nan Ch'uan said they would go on if they could speak Truth. Kuei Tsung and Ma Ku understood and immediately expressed Truth in different ways. Simultaneously, however, their different ways of speaking Truth returned to the same home. Like many rivers streaming to the ocean, they returned and became One.

Living in vow

IN BUDDHISM A SPIRITUAL LIFE requires the practice of taking a vow. Mahayana Buddhists take the vow of the bodhisattva, which has four parts: to taste Truth, to save all beings, to master the teachings of the Buddha, to accomplish the Buddha Way.

In Zen we speak of living in vow. This means we attend wholeheartedly to the activities of everyday life. When it is time to get up, we just get up. When it is time to wash the dishes, we just wash the dishes. But you might wonder, what is the difference between living in vow and just forming a habit?

We form habits every day—watching TV, going to school, going to work. Habits are linked to our desires. If there is no satisfaction in a habit, you won't continue it for long. Living in vow, on the other hand, is to carry out your routines with no sense of attempting to satisfy your individual desires. Under all circumstances, beyond your likes or dislikes, you have to carry on. It's pretty hard, but it's very important. This is the difference between habit and vow. The difference is total.

This applies not only in Buddhism but in other practices as well. For example, if you want to have a peaceful life through the practice of yoga, you have to exercise daily. Day by day, under all circumstances, you form the routine of yoga practice. Slowly your heart and mind will then change, and your spiritual life will develop.

The changes that occur through spiritual practice are not really your business. If you make them your business, you will try to change your life directly. If you try to change your life directly, no matter how long you work at it, you will not satisfy yourself. So, if you truly want to change your life, you should just form the routine of doing small things, day by day. Then your life will be changed beyond your expectations. If you practice continuously, day after day, you will become a peaceful, gentle, and harmonious person. There is no explanation for this.

I have heard an interesting story about how a famous psychologist in Japan cured a young girl after she suffered a nervous breakdown. The girl was from a wealthy family, and the psychologist met her regularly. But he didn't do or say anything. He just sat with her. One day, as he was sitting with her, the girl peed on the floor right in front of him. He was a very neat gentleman, and he was dressed in a very fine suit. But the moment she did this, he immediately took the beautiful handkerchief from his breast pocket and, without comment, cleaned up after her.

In time she completely recovered. She later recalled this incident, because she was very impressed by the psychologist's actions that day. Without any hesitation, he just mopped the floor with his fresh, neat handkerchief. There is no way to explain why she recovered. He didn't do anything. He only cleaned up after her during this one incident. But she could feel something very soft, gentle, and magnanimous coming from each pore of his body. She really respected him.

Have you ever met such a person? The moment you meet such people you feel relief just by their presence or their smile. Such people actually do exist in the world. How can we cultivate and nurture this kind of character in ourselves? It is not done through any intellectual process. This kind of change only comes about through living in vow, through taking care of your life. If you just practice the little things, day by day, without attempting to satisfy any of your individual desires—if you just do this continuously—your magnanimous personality will become manifest.

Living in vow is like taking a trip down the Mississippi River. If you go to the center of the river, there is no need for any extra effort. If you go to the center of your life, the river of your life will carry you. If you practice in this way, you will find a natural rhythm to your life. Start with taking care of the little things in your life on an everyday basis, and eventually you will get to the middle of the river.

Before you reach the middle of the stream, practice feels hard. Most people give up. But they give up only because they don't see their life in the long range. They want results, right now. Life is very hard on us if we take this attitude. We become nervous, irritable, and cold-hearted.

If you learn to take a long-range view of life, you will continue to practice routinely, and you will get to the middle of the stream. Then, without any extra effort, your body and mind will move along in peace and harmony. A sense of gentleness, generosity, and magnanimity will come forth from each pore of your body. Your vow will have become your life.

Dharma and play

IN BUDDHISM THE SANSKRIT TERM *Dharma* has three meanings: the ultimate principle of existence, the phenomena of experience, and the teaching about the nature of things. These three meanings work together. For example, without phenomena—without mundane human life—the ultimate principle can never manifest. And unless it is transmitted, the Truth will not be realized.

Dogen Zenji said that to listen to the Dharma is to be transformed through the process of playing freely. "To transform" doesn't mean to change your body or your mental capacities. And this play is not done for any purpose. To play freely is to have full commitment to just playing.

Wholehearted play has the power to transform your life. It's like the art of diving into the ocean from atop the cliff at Acapulco. How beautiful it is! The diver doesn't measure as he recreates his life while diving. He's right in the middle of it. Like so, to listen to the Dharma is to let your conscious mind disport itself freely. This is the creative life.

But *your* creative life is not your business. It can't be held by your consciousness. Other people can feel how beautiful it is. They can see it—just like watching the diver as he dives.

In the case of zazen, you have to practice for your whole life. It doesn't matter whether you are a beginner or an adept. From beginning to end, we have to just practice. That way we can produce a life that is ever fresh and new.

In order to disport yourself freely in the Dharma, you must be bighearted. In each moment, your heart must produce a new life. This new life must be transmittable. In other words, you can't keep it to yourself. You must convey it to others.

From day to day we learn by digesting the culture of people who lived before us. We then have the responsibility to transmit what we have learned to the next generation.

To digest what you learn in life takes time. It also takes warm communication with others—not only with people, but with trees, birds, winter, and all sentient beings. But as you digest and learn, you can begin to disport yourself freely in the Dharma.

You can easily live in vivid reality from day to day. Then, very naturally, in everything you do, you will express your deep appreciation of life. This deep appreciation you feel for all life is a treasure, and you will want to transmit this treasure, this life of freedom, to the next generation.

Knowing the whole

WE CAN SAY THAT BUDDHIST PRACTICE has two aspects: to constantly seek Truth and to go into the human world.

If you want to be a pianist, devote yourself to studying and practicing the piano. This is the mind that seeks Truth. But though you may eventually reach a lofty stage as a musician, it is not good enough. You have to descend into the human world as well. Your life, your presence, your personality must touch people's hearts directly. This means you have to go beyond being a pianist.

It is relatively easy to teach people to be musicians, but it is not so easy to teach them how to go beyond being a musician. If you would teach this to others, your mind must be based on compassion. When you teach, you have to pierce the human heart and take away the flag of ego. So your compassion must extend beyond the words you use. Then your penetrating words will teach and not injure.

To teach people how to go beyond, your attitude must be soft yet stable, like the center of a ball. No matter where it rolls, the ball's center never changes. You must always stand alone and unmoved. You can't get carried away by the eight winds of gain or loss, public defamation or eulogy, private praise or ridicule, sorrow or joy. Most people are easily tossed about by these winds. If people praise you, you smile. My teacher often scolded me, but once he praised me, and I smiled. Immediately he said, "How stupid you are!" I didn't understand at the time how these winds can get us into trouble.

Although those who seek Truth stand in the middle of the eight winds, they are alone and unmoved. When someone attacks, they don't fight back. So when you see others flex their muscles in front of you, just accept them. If you fight with them, *you* will show your muscle. There is no end to such fighting. Nor is there ever any sense of victory or defeat.

When somebody attacks, you should just withdraw. But to "withdraw" is not to withdraw. It doesn't mean defeat. If somebody puts you down, be noble. Remain gentle, compassionate, and patient. If you can do this, you can realize great freedom. This is nirvana.

Some people misunderstand Zen. They think of it as "unteaching." They say it is to know water by drinking it, and that that is the whole matter. But this is to know only a part of the universe. Even if you drink the water, there are still many things you don't know.

Religious practice must include the whole world. Even though you cannot know everything, you Know. You mustn't panic just because you cannot know all the details. Most people try to get a clear answer before they act, but you can't always get one. But if you say yes to something, then you can act with confidence. This spirit is very important. Every day, step by step, you have to walk in a stately manner. In this way you can come to Know the Whole.

Firewood and ashes

IN THE *Genjokoan* Dogen Zenji wrote:

> Once firewood turns to ash, the ash cannot turn back to being firewood. Still, one should not take the view that it is ashes afterward and firewood before. One should realize that although firewood is at the dharmastage of firewood, and that this is possessed of before and after, the firewood is beyond before and after.

This passage from the *Genjokoan* is not easy to understand if we read it in our usual frame of mind. It forces us to see what we have never seen before and to hear what we have never heard before.

Dogen's teaching doesn't explain Buddhism philosophically or psychologically. Yet his religious thinking is very deep. Although to some his writings seem to be philosophical, from the start his words point directly to actual practice. Instead of endless analyzing and synthesizing, Dogen's teaching points to everyday life. In Dogen a refined, natural, religious thought emerges within the context of dynamic practice.

Most people think that religion is a matter of believing in something—perhaps a divine being, unknowable and untouchable. But Dogen's teaching is not about belief. It is about *understanding*—understanding what is ungraspable and inconceivable.

Of course, "ungraspable" or "inconceivable" are themselves just ideas, pointers to what is still utterable. Dogen's way is not to form some *idea* of what is really inconceivable and ungraspable, because to hold on to an *idea* creates a lot of trouble for us. Dogen goes beyond the utterable, until there is nothing to say and nothing to grasp. He worked human experience until he knew directly the ungraspable and inconceivable. He didn't give up until he reached the ineffable.

If religion were merely an explanation, it would not show us the full range of human experience. Therefore we must not attach either to an intellectual understanding of religion or to our emotional response to it. This is not our usual way, but it is crucial to having religious insight.

Dogen's example of firewood illuminates this point quite well. The common idea that firewood turns to ash is easy to grasp. That ash does not turn back into being firewood is also easy to understand. But Dogen says we shouldn't take the view that ash is afterward and firewood is before.

Why does he say this? Because we commonly think of firewood and ashes as they appear in time. We believe that the firewood we see in the present, when burned in the future, turns to ashes. But Dogen Zenji says this is not a very deep understanding of what goes on. It is too simplistic. Actually, it is contradictory. Although this instant has "before" and "after," what we are calling firewood is beyond before and after. In this context, "beyond" means to completely cut off our notion of time—that is, to completely cut off our ideas of before and after. Firewood does not exist through time. Like all things, it can only exist *now*.

When Dogen speaks of the "dharma-stage of firewood," he means that that stage is the whole universe. Only in the realm of the Whole is there before and after. Thus before and after exist only when firewood is seen to exist in the realm of the Whole.

Our usual sense of before and after is associated with time, which we see as flowing from past to present to future. We tend to think of time as a continuum—that is, we see past, present, and future as being connected. But Dogen speaks of each moment as being independent, although always manifest within the Whole. Thus each moment, though absolutely distinct, is simultaneously the entire universe.

But how does a single moment become the whole universe? Time is just motion, but it is motion with nothing moving. Time has no form apart from space. And all things that appear exist in becoming, in movement from moment to moment. In other words, your life is time. It exists only in the coming and going of this moment, and nowhere else. In this realm of arising and ceasing, all beings are manifest.

This moment—now—is not our idea of this moment, which is necessarily separate from the next moment. We cannot *think* this moment—we have to *see* it. And we can only *see* this moment by going deeply into it. Just as you must go to the bottom of the ocean if you want to touch its floor, you must go deeply into this moment if you want to touch its depth. In touching the bottom of *this* moment, there is no idea of "this moment." In the vividness of *this* moment, time and space are one. Thus, our individual life and the whole universe can be seen simultaneously in this moment.

The question is, how can *we* see this? How can we see the transfiguration of *this moment* as the Whole? How can we see ourselves as the Whole? Dogen doesn't bother to explain this. It needs no explanation, because it can be *seen* directly. Instead he emphasizes that this transfiguration occurs in the functioning of this moment. For example, when you put your palms together in the gesture we call *gassho*, that *gassho* is energy—it is a living form. In other words, this formed energy appears in a certain space, which we call *gassho*.

Energy can take many forms. Sometimes it takes the form of drinking a cup of tea. Sometimes it takes the form of zazen. But in *doing* zazen, the *idea* of zazen is secondary. The *idea* of *you* is secondary. There is just zazen. In drinking tea, there is just drinking tea. The ideas of "tea" and "cup" and "you" are secondary. They are just frozen ideas.

In the very moment you do something, the whole universe happens. In other words, now is made manifest by the fact that when you meet something, it meets you. When you meet zazen, zazen meets you. The free and pure nature of this moment is thus revealed.

Doing zazen is dynamic practice. It is the pure functioning of this moment. It is not an idea. Such practice is undefiled. Apart from the pure nature of undefiled practice, you cannot Know Reality. However, even if you ignore such practice, strictly speaking, all beings still live in accordance with Truth. This is why we have the opportunity, and the capacity, to wake up.

We usually don't see this Reality of all beings working together, so it is hard to live in accord with it. Instead we live according to a fragmented view of reality. We live according to our ideas of this and that in a world of give and take. This is why it is very difficult for us to understand Buddhist teachings. For example, when I meet with a student and the student tells me something or asks me a question, often I am expected to make some immediate response. The student tries to get something from me. But this is not a real meeting. A real meeting offers no response. It is just this moment arising. If you beat a drum to assert yourself, no matter how long you hit the drum, the universe will not respond to you. Your expectations kill the possibility. But if you practice with no expectation, the universe responds. Therefore, to truly *see* a teacher—or anybody—means you cannot expect a certain response. If you have a preconceived idea of your meeting, there is actually no meeting.

"No response" really means to *just see. Just see, just do.* When you meet zazen, *just meet.* We are not used to entering into an activity without expectations, so this is really difficult. Still, an understanding of this way of living can be found, but not through the intellect. It can be found in the practice of this moment.

You have to say something

ANYTHING YOU THINK ABOUT Buddha-nature is just some idea in your mind. But Buddha-nature is not something we can grasp. In this sense, there is no Buddha-nature.

We want to know if Buddha-nature exists or not. But no matter how long we discuss it, there is no end to the subject. What is there to say about Buddha-nature? Nothing. The same is true of whatever aspect of human life you pick up: finally there is nothing to say.

A monk once asked his master, "What is the essence of Buddhism?" The master said, "Step forward from the top of a hundred-foot pole."

How can we go forward from the top of the pole? We will

die. Can we go backward? No, we cannot. What, then, does it mean to step forward from the top of a hundred-foot pole?

Though we are not always conscious of it, we actually face this question daily. As we do become aware of it, we finally ask ourselves, What is life? But there is nothing to say. Just silence. This silence is Buddha-nature, or Suchness, or Emptiness.

Though everyone experiences this silence, we usually don't notice it because our minds are very busy. Sooner or later, though, we all realize its presence. But then we ask, "What is this silence? How can I speak of it? Do I just keep my mouth shut?" No, I don't think so. Even if you don't say anything, there is still a problem. Silence—Buddha-nature—is not something apart from your life. It compels you to speak. That is why the Zen master had to speak. He had to say something. He had to speak from that silence—from Buddha-nature.

When you really understand your life—when you really understand what makes it possible for all beings to exist—there is nothing to say. You just keep silent. But still you have to do something. This is why I always tell you to keep your mouth shut and act with true heart. Buddha-nature is the state of your life as you stand atop a hundred-foot pole. You have to do something. Take one step.

_____ Expressing true heart

THE CHINESE PEOPLE of ancient times expressed spiritual joyfulness naturally through dance. We express such joyfulness in other ways as well, but strictly speaking, all such expression is the same. But if our expression is offered in words or deeds, we might not understand, because the joyfulness is *behind* the form through which it is being expressed.

Eating and sleeping can be expressions of religious joyfulness. We might not believe this, but it's true. In Zen we don't exaggerate the expression of joy, but we show it quietly in how we take care of our everyday routine. This way of expressing spiritual joyfulness is different from more familiar forms. Still, at bottom it's the same. Each form must be expressed whole-heartedly. When our activity comes from the bottom of our life, it's dancing.

If joyfulness is expressed just physically, it is not true joyful-ness. Joyfulness must come from behind our physical expres-sions. This is not easy to see, but it makes an impression. In it, there is teaching.

Zen teachers in China and Japan don't explain very much. They just give a simple word, or they just walk away, offering no verbal explanation. This is why their teachings are very dif-ficult to understand. But the important point is that this kind of teaching is direct. It doesn't come through intellection.

Most people are used to having things explained. But all we get in this way is the surface of human life. Explaining things according to common sense doesn't always work. It is very dif-ficult to see what is profound and deep through such ordinary teaching. The real meaning dies. But most of us are not patient enough to learn to see what is beneath the surface. It takes time to touch what is deep. This is why we have to practice patience: we have to see what is behind physical and verbal expressions.

To understand this, your intention must be very strong. You must seek this understanding with complete sincerity for a long time. But if you are patient and sincere, even one word can touch the heart. The specific word itself is not so impor-tant. If used properly, it can carry profound meaning. Yet it is very difficult to say just what that meaning is. It is like trying to explain how one awakens.

Later on, of course, we can write a story describing the expe-rience. But people still won't understand, because they don't understand what is behind the words.

Our actual experience is like meeting a moose on a country road. Even though there is nothing strange about it, you are immediately impressed. The moose is just a moose, yet you feel something immediately. It is very difficult to grasp the total picture of this scene from someone who later recalls it and tells it as a story.

The ancient Zen masters never gave up wanting to understand the Truth of *this moment*. They would seek it constantly, under all circumstances. This is true religious intention. To acquire peace and harmony in this moment, you must seek it twenty-four hours a day.

Today we are always soaking our bodies in the nice warm bathwater of modern civilization. We might say that we should share our lives with poor people, that we should give something to them. Meanwhile, we're in a nice warm bathtub. Then, *if* we have some spare time or some spare change, we say, "Let's share it with others." Consciously or unconsciously, we protect ourselves first. How, then, are we to truly understand the lives of the ancients, who suffered severe deprivation? They *had* to face poverty, and not by choice.

We might talk a lot about compassion and kindness, but there is very little practice of it. We just exercise our ideas about these things. We're all talk. Day after day, we just talk. And then we think we understand.

But without practice there is no understanding. For example, really drinking a cup of tea is not anything you can see—it is not an idea. To drink a cup of tea in peace and harmony means that nothing hinges on drinking a cup of tea—not you, not the cup, not the tea, not even the drinking of tea. Then, very naturally, all things that surround you and the cup cooperate with your drinking a cup of tea. At that time you feel stable, and you can really drink.

You have to pay attention to this very moment where you drink the cup of tea. You and the cup and the tea and all beings join in the act of drinking tea. At that time drinking tea becomes peace and harmony. This is to express our true heart.

When there's nothing to say

IF YOU STUDY BUDDHISM, you will hear a lot about the idea of reincarnation. I don't say that you should ignore it, but you shouldn't attach to it either. We easily become attached to ideas of reincarnation, karma, enlightenment, nirvana, and a lot of other fancy religious notions. We become greedy. We might want a peek at heaven, but then we'll be caught by heaven.

We all have our own peculiarities, our own uniqueness. No one can really imitate another. Usually, however, we take a very egoistic view. We don't know how to nurture our actual life. This is why we might attach to the idea of reincarnation. But if you attach to the idea of reincarnation, you will never find perfect freedom.

What do we mean by reincarnation? If I said I am a reincarnation of Dogen, how could I be free now? I would be nothing but an imitation of Dogen's life. Life is not an imitation. Dogen is like no one else. No one can stand in for him. Dogen's life is Dogen's life, in perfect freedom. And your life is your life, also in perfect freedom.

There was once a Japanese prince who was well loved and praised by everyone. He didn't really walk two or three feet off the ground, but everyone felt that he did. They couldn't praise him enough, but all the words that were offered couldn't hit the mark. So the people looked for ways to praise him more. Finally they began to say that he was the reincarnation of the Buddha. But Buddha is Buddha. The prince is the prince. One cannot replace the other. If we see the prince not as the prince but as someone else, then we can't really appreciate the greatness of the prince in his own right. If the Buddha is not the Buddha, then we cannot understand his life either.

Only you can live your life. So our practice is to be genuine, not an imitation of someone else. Look at your life. In Truth you can't put any kind of label on it. Are you stupid? No. Are you great? No. Are you completely average? No. We think we have to supply answers to these kinds of questions, that we have to pin down who we are. But we only have to live our lives, day by day. And only you can live yours.

But what are you? If you really study yourself, you will hear a strange sound. There's a cry. It's the sound of the world, the sound of everyone. It comes from inside you. Inside yourself you will hear the quiet cries of the world. To hear this sound means you really want to know how to live.

Should we emphasize the teaching of reincarnation? The more you think about it, the more you create a gap. Your body is here, but your mind is far away—gone into the past, into the future, lost in imagining a world after death, imagining heaven and hell. This is more or less what we all do. That's why, when we closely observe the world in this present moment, we hear screaming. If you look at yourself with a true heart, very naturally you will hear the cry of the world.

We have to go beyond notions of reincarnation, karma, nirvana, and enlightenment. This is the goal of Buddhism. This means to come back to yourself and how you are living now. The question is, how should we live? How can we take care of the cries of the world, which we hear when we observe ourselves closely?

Dogen Zenji said: "People ask, 'What is the Buddha?' An icicle forming in fire." The idea of an icicle in fire seems impossible. Nevertheless, this is the reality in which we live.

What *is* Buddha? Even Buddha doesn't know. We can't pin him down. We can't catch him in our grasp. If we say he is a wonderful, divine being of some sort who watches us from somewhere far off, this is not Buddha. In Truth, Buddha is fully alive within life itself. Buddha is very quiet. He doesn't appear as an image in our minds. Buddha is Reality itself.

Today Buddhism in the United States is developing well. But what is Buddhism? What is a real Buddhist? And why should we study Buddhism? There are many such questions, but when we try to pin down answers, we are confused.

Such questions are not just limited to Buddhism. Why study Christianity? What do you really know about God? And how much do you understand about what you don't understand about God? Finally there's nothing to say. Even though you say you are a Christian or a Buddhist, all names become a blur. Though I say, "I am a Zen priest," what does this mean? There's nothing to say. Still, even in the middle of nothing to say, we can pay attention to *this moment*. This is all we have to do.

Beyond our likes and dislikes, we have to pay attention to how we actually live. Right in the middle of good and bad, right and wrong, our lives go on constantly.

Whatever kind of label you put on your life, or the lives of others—good, bad, or neutral—there is always a cry. If you become happy, right in the middle of happiness there's a cry. If you become unhappy, there's still a cry. Even if you say, "I don't care," right in the middle of your not caring, there's a cry. Even when you sleep like a log, there's still a cry. Whatever you do, there's always a cry.

Your life is dynamic. It never forms into anything particular, such as being enlightened or being the reincarnation of Buddha. There is nothing particular to do; there is nothing particular to say. Nevertheless, if you pay attention to your life as it is, you will discover that right in the middle of "nothing particular to do," there is something you must do. Right in the middle of "nothing particular to say," you have to say something. Observe closely. Be fully alive in each moment. This is the real way to live.

Zen in Everyday Life

To PRACTICE ZEN IN EVERYDAY LIFE you must pay attention to the existence of others. To practice our way, you have to practice with all sentient beings. Zen in everyday life and everyday life in Zen are not two different things. They are one, just like a Japanese folding fan.

This kind of fan consists of two parts—an upper part that folds, and a lower part that pivots. The pivot is like the original teaching of Zen—practicing full concentration and no attachment. But it doesn't make sense to think of a fan that is just a pivot without a part that unfolds. The pivot must be able to unfold into a fan. In other words, the pivot must be open to daily life—not just your daily life, but the daily life of others as well. In this way, the fan as a whole—that is, your practice—works pretty well. It will help you and others to become one with the earth, with nature, with all things.

Zen teaching must unfold like this fan. When Zen is unfolded, immediately there appear many dimensions to life. Zen teaching must be alive in all of them.

As I said, Zen teaches full concentration and no attachment.

This might seem paradoxical. Full concentration means to throw yourself completely away. This sounds negative: forget yourself and jump into zazen. But this negative expression of human life manifests in the affirmative—that is, in no attachment. No attachment means peaceful, harmonious life.

If you study Zen, you will find many seemingly paradoxical expressions. For instance, we say, "See the flower without seeing it." But how can you do that? How can you see the flower if you are not seeing it?

Dogen Zenji says, "When you let go of everything, you get everything in your hand." This is the real teaching of Zen. The point is not to make you confused. Explanations of Zen seem paradoxical, but Zen itself is not paradoxical. You can experience this directly.

Why do we practice full concentration and no attachment? Do you believe it is because you have to train yourself and deepen your life? That's just part of the reason. The practice of full concentration and no attachment is not just for yourself; it is for all sentient beings. Do you believe that you can have a clear and serene mind in zazen while ignoring the lives of others? You cannot. The sense that your practice is just your individual practice is really egoistic. You ignore people who, like you, want to have peaceful and harmonious lives. You only focus on *your* peaceful, harmonious life. This is a big mistake.

During World War II, the Japanese government used to motivate people to throw themselves into the war. "When you go to war, concentrate on killing people. This will bring success. This will support Japan." But does Japan exist alone in the universe? No, of course not.

Don't misunderstand Zen teachings. A partial understanding can be very dangerous. You might then use Zen teachings to support your ego. If you would love Japan, you must love Japan and America and all countries, regardless of what race and culture their people belong to. You have to love all human beings. *Then* you can put Zen teachings into practice in the world. *Then* Zen teaching can really work in peace and harmony.

Zen in everyday life is based on what we call living in vow. I have a calligraphy of four vows on my wall. In English it reads:

> Sentient beings are numberless; I vow to save them.
> Desires are inexhaustible; I vow to put an end to them.
> The Dharmas are boundless; I vow to master them.
> The Buddha Way is unsurpassable; I vow to attain it.

These vows are very important for us. To live in vow is not to live by your own will or volition. These vows come from greater depths than personal volition or will. If you keep these vows in your daily life, you are what is called a bodhisattva.

The determination to live in vow is like springwater coming from the ground. You can't stop it. If you understand the total picture of human life, these vows come up very naturally, like springwater, to save all sentient beings. To the intellect, it seems impossible to save all sentient beings. But actually, it is possible.

When we say the vows in English, we say, "I vow." But bodhisattvas don't assert the "I." The bodhisattva's life is completely without subject or object. This is full concentration. Thus a bodhisattva is not a bodhisattva. This bodhisattva is really, fully alive.

To become a bodhisattva without the frame of a bodhisattva—to let yourself be fully alive—do not concentrate in the realm of ideas, philosophy, or psychology. Don't even concentrate in the realm of like or dislike. Just be alive. This is Zen in everyday life.

The Art of Zazen

ZAZEN IS SITTING MEDITATION. *Za* means "to sit," and *zen* is tranquillity. In Chinese, the character *za* is a picture of two people sitting on the earth. This means we have to sit zazen with others—not just with other people, but with all beings.

You can't sit zazen alone—that is, you can't sit within an egoistic, selfish territory that is all your own. It's impossible. To sit zazen, you must open yourself to the universe. To sit zazen with all beings is for all beings to sit zazen with you.

We have to make our best effort to sit zazen without expecting anything extra. If you expect something from your zazen—even slightly—you can't do your best. You have created two goals: zazen and the purpose of zazen. If you want to do zazen, just do zazen.

Intellectually, you want to know what zazen is. So you ask, "What is the purpose of zazen?" "What is the result?" "What meaning is there in it?" But if you simply jump into zazen, with full participation and attention, with no separation between you and zazen, then, very naturally, you can see some result.

If you do zazen after hearing that it makes you calm, then

you expect to be calm when you sit zazen. But when you actually sit zazen, you discover your mind is very busy. You are not calm at all. You are confused, because you acquired an intellectual understanding of zazen before you actually experienced it. And so you ask, "Why should I do this?" When this happens, what you must do is just forget any expectations you have about zazen and just sit.

There are three basic points to zazen. First is harmonizing the body; second is harmonizing the mind; third is harmonizing the breath.

You must sit up straight. If you slouch, your posture is very unstable. It seems to be comfortable to sit that way, but it isn't really. Your body is stressed, and you can't breathe very well. Your heart and intestines can't function well. It is also harder to keep your balance. As a result, your body as a whole becomes agitated, and you can't sit for very long. Sitting on a cushion, your body forms a sort of pyramid, with your center of gravity right in the middle. This makes your posture very stable. Even if you fall asleep, you will not fall over. So, even though you may not feel comfortable at first, sit up straight.

Harmonizing the body also means you have to arrange your external circumstances. The room you do zazen in should not be messy or dirty. It shouldn't be too bright or too dark, too hot or too cold and drafty. Make your external circumstances pleasant and comfortable.

To begin zazen, cross your legs by placing your right foot on your left thigh or your left foot on your right thigh. Or sit in the full lotus, with both your feet on your thighs. If you do the full lotus, your weight is on three points—your two knees and your buttocks. If you can't put either foot on your thigh, that's okay. But it is still important to have your knees on the mat and your hips on the round cushion. You can also kneel with a cushion directly under your buttocks. Just make sure your weight is on the same three points—your two knees and your buttocks.

Next, put your hands on your knees with the palms up. Take a deep breath through your mouth. As you inhale, lean backward a bit from the base of your spine. Do this slowly with full attention. Then, as you exhale, lean forward again and return to a stable, upright position, with your back straight.

Next, as you exhale, lean far to the right, dropping your head toward your right shoulder and stretching out the left side of your body. Then, as you inhale, bring your body back to the center. Then, slowly lean your body to the left as you exhale, dropping your head toward your left shoulder and stretching out the right side of your body. Repeat this process of leaning to one side and then the other several times, each time leaning a little bit less. It's important to do this physical and mental preparation before you sit.

Next, place your left hand, palm up, on your upturned right palm, thumb tips just touching and forming an oval. Your hands should not be loose or tense. They should make a soft, gentle form, which is called the cosmic mudra. This form is a symbol of the universe. We can't exist without the universe, so we acknowledge it in our posture.

We must appreciate the universe. It unifies all beings in peace and harmony. When we put our two hands together in the cosmic mudra, it represents two beings sitting in the universe. You have to sit with a true feeling of the harmony of the whole.

The universe that you form with your hands must be one with your center of gravity—that is, it must rest just in front of your lower abdomen, so that your thumbs are placed just at or below your navel.

Hold your arms forward just a bit at the elbows, so they don't touch the sides of your body. We sometimes say it's like holding a raw egg under each armpit: not so tight that you crush it; not so loose that you drop it.

Push your lower back forward. This is a little hard if you have never done it before, but it will help to support your back. Then straighten your upper back and your head. Keep your neck parallel with the wall. Then, without moving your neck, pull in your chin. Sit as though you're pushing up the ceiling with the top of the back of your head. Very naturally, your back will straighten up.

Without leaning to the right or to the left, or forward or backward, keep your body straight. Then cast your eyes to the floor. Look at a wide area; don't pick out a specific spot. The area you're looking at should be about the same distance in front of you as your eyes are above the floor. Your eyes should be slightly open. If you close your eyes, you will experience visual images. They might be fun, but you will create distractions for yourself. If you open your eyes too wide, that's also trouble. Your mind will scatter. As you begin zazen, if it's difficult to take care of your mind, you can close your eyes for a little while. But as soon as possible, you should open them again.

Next, bring your teeth and lips together. Your tongue should touch the roof of your mouth, but just naturally. Keep your mouth closed. Breathe through your nose, and let the breath go down to your abdomen. Breathe slowly. When you have the proper posture, your breath goes in and out very naturally. It will then go all the way down to your lower abdomen without stopping. If you pay attention to your breath, your respiration rate will become slower than usual.

Sometimes you will have a problem with your breath, perhaps because of too much tension in the lower abdomen. If you do have trouble, just breathe as naturally as you can for a while. Don't worry about how well you're doing. Forget judgment. If you see that the situation with your breath is not good, just relax and let your breath return to normal. If you become irritated because you're trying to control your breath, just let it go. Your breath is naturally always changing, according to your emotions, your feelings, your physical conditions, and your external circumstances.

Usually your mind is very busy. It's just like a monkey, leaping about here and there. So you must take care of it. Harmonize your mind. Let your mind sit in zazen. Don't let it go. If you let it go, it runs wild. Let whatever kind of mind you have—monkey mind, good mind, calm mind—let it sit with you. To do this, your mind should be with your breath. When you inhale, concentrate on your lower abdomen moving out. When you exhale, notice your abdomen moving in.

Sometimes you can reverse it. This practice is particularly good if you feel sleepy or lazy, or if you lose your spirit. In that case, practice breathing so that when you inhale your lower abdomen goes in a little bit, and when you exhale your lower abdomen goes out. This might help wake you up.

Your mind should be with your breath. Often, however, it will leave. At that time, bring it back to your zazen. Very often your mind is like a wild kid—always running about. Then you should be just like a mother, always bringing the kid back. I don't know how often you will have to do this—maybe for the whole period of zazen.

When you see your mind going out and coming back, going out and coming back, you will eventually ask, "What is zazen?" But don't worry. All you have to do is learn to see where your mind is and, if it goes out, bring it back. This is all we have to do. This is the art of zazen.

When zazen is over, release your hands and put them on your knees, palms facing upward. Lean to the right, then to the left, going from small motions to larger ones, leaning a little more each time. Exhale as you lean and inhale as you bring your body back to the center. Repeat this until your swings are very large; then come back to the center and stop.

You shouldn't act too abruptly after zazen. Move slowly. Release your legs and stretch out. Then slowly stand up.

Through zazen you can learn to be present, beyond your likes and dislikes. Even though you sit zazen every day, ego can still be a problem. You can become proud of your practice. Wherever you go, you may insist on doing zazen. Or you may kick out anyone who interferes with your zazen. Or you might stop caring about your family, your schooling, your job, your office, and just care about your zazen. Sometimes people do these things, but it's all just egoism. This is not right practice.

If this kind of thing happens, all you have to do is just forget it. Day by day, just do zazen quietly—without any ideas or expectations. Avoid doing zazen for show. Just keep zazen modestly, as a religious practice.

If you attach to the good experiences you get through zazen, you will create expectations of enlightenment. Then you won't be peaceful, because you will just want more, more, more. You will want a better life, and so your mind will be kept very busy. If you get the idea that zazen is wonderful, this is just the experience of wanting more. It's not zazen.

If you are confused in your zazen, you are not in peace. But peace is exactly what zazen is. If you just realize that all you have to do is to harmonize your mind, your body, and your breath, then you will learn to be present beyond your likes and dislikes. Furthermore, you will realize great vitality. You will know true peace and tranquillity. This helps not just you but others as well. Just experience zazen as perfect harmony— harmony that must be shared with all beings.

Zazen is to realize exactly who you are. This is all you have to do.